Best Wishes
Sharron
3·10·96

Jump Jockeys Don't Cry

I dedicate this book to my
Mother, Thelma.
We have been on a long journey together
and it is not over yet!

S HARRON   M URGATROYD

Romney Publications

Published by

Romney Publications
Graseby House · Exning Road · Newmarket · Suffolk CB8 0AU

First published 1996

© Sharron Murgatroyd 1996

© This edition Romney Publications

ISBN 0 9528566 0 3 Hardback
ISBN 0 9528566 1 1 Paperback

Designed and Typeset by
Equine Veterinary Journal Ltd.

Printed by
Caligraving Ltd · Thetford · Norfolk · England

Front cover:
Fiefdom taking a mint

Back cover:
Songbird Miracle, Fakenham 1991 (P.H. Photography)

Contents

Invictus

OoO

Out of the night that covers me
Black as the pit from pole to pole
I thank whatever Gods may be
For my unconquerable soul

In the fell clutch of circumstance
I have not winced nor cried aloud
Under the bludgeonings of chance
My head is bloody, but unbowed

Beyond this place of wrath and tears
Looms but the horror of the shade
And yet the menace of the years
Finds and shall find me, unafraid

It matters not how strait the gate
How charged with punishments the scroll
I am the master of my fate;
I am the captain of my soul

OoO

William Henley

Foreword by Brough Scott

Sharron's book is not just a tremendous accomplishment. It is a tremendous book. To have gone through the hassle and trauma of getting her story into print would have been effort enough in all our eyes. But Sharron has done much, much more than that. She has done what we professional writers almost always fail to do. She has made the story and the heartache come screaming off the page.

She has taken you into her life from the very beginning. From the Yorkshire childhood with its unhappy changing of the family deal. From the early connection with ponies to formative years at the Dickinson's Gisburn academy, and then to riding the Newmarket roller coaster in the racing game. From the first straining thoroughbred canter to the obsessive drive for actual victory on the track. From easy going stable staff teenage days to a young woman's agony when a relationship runs on the rocks. And then one hurdle too brave and the greatest agony of all. Read this book. You will not be the same when you have finished.

Obviously much of this has an uncomfortable ring about it. There are times when you wish you could smile in sympathy and skip the page just as we all too often pass a disabled person with a cheery greeting rather than stop to actually hear what they have to say. But Sharron's towering success is that her words hold the attention. However dreadfully difficult her predicament may have been, she has the ability to take you there too. You will not enjoy this part. But neither will you want to avoid it.

For starting this story you are entering a life in the whole. For those of us long-toothed in the racing circus you would have thought Sharron's telling of her particular pursuit of the jockey's dream would be no more than another spin of a fairly hackneyed tale. But here are vivid, candid pictures of people, places, and of the horses too. We understand their talents, their failings, their hopes and fears, as if we are at Sharron's side. Which of course we are. For her achievement is to take us there. And not just we bow-legged so called experts. Anyone can appreciate this work. Anyone with a heart.

She has been to pits of pain and despair beyond most of our imaginings. But she has been somewhere else. She has been to the country of the mind where truth lives on the page. Sharron already has much to be proud of. This book should top the lot.

A further word from John Francome

"Didn't we have a lovely time the day we went to Bangor". The opening line to one of the most trivial songs ever recorded could not have been less appropriate for Sharron Murgatroyd. A fall from a moderate hurdler at the tiny Welsh Racecourse on the opening day of the 1991 jump season left her with a neck broken in five places, and the numbing news that she would never walk again. This book bares the thoughts and emotions of a life that was far from easy, even before her accident. It should be on the bedside table of every able bodied person as a guarantee to remind us all, just how lucky we are. To put any problems into perspective. Sharron isn't the only person I know who is paralysed, but she is one of the bravest. Fate may have taken away her mobility, and nipped a promising riding career in the bud, but in its place a talent for writing and poetry has blossomed, and her cheerfulness remains as an example to us all. A careful read of this might change your life, almost as much as "A day at Bangor" changed hers.

Strength
(for my Mother)

oOo

I know your love is greater than mine
But I've lost some deepness
As I live a new life
My love and my hate
Lay side by side
While I fight... with strength
To live my life

I know your pain is different to mine
But we both must be strong
And live a life
The love and the hate
Can stand side by side
While we... with strength
Keep our pride

I know your life has been longer than mine
But you have survived
No need to cry
To love and to hate
Must be put aside
While you... with strength
Live your life

I know your courage is the same as mine
And we will fight
Till the end of time
Your love and your hate
Leave by the door
While... with strength
We strive to conquer all

oOo

Sharron Murgatroyd

CHAPTER ONE

August 2nd 1991

The alarm sounded twice as loud as usual: 4.10am; I hadn't slept much during the night. The past nine months had been filled with so many different emotions but, after seven and a half years of sharing my life with a very special person, it had come to a very sad and abrupt end. I hurt inside like nobody else ever could and the one thing that kept me going was riding horses, riding races, riding winners…

My body ached in some sort of protest as I made my way to the bathroom. The next procedure was to weigh myself – it was becoming quite an obsession but I had it under control. There was no need to worry about the weight I was jumping today, and tomorrow at Newmarket I was set to carry well over 10st on the Henry Cecil trained *Snickersnee*, whom I'd already steered to victory once this season. The scales read 8st 6lb, which pleased me, while the heartache of the night began to subside. I felt fit and strong as I quickly laid out a pair of white cotton pedal pushers, navy top with matching sweat shirt, and navy and white shoes. They would be just right for the first day of the jump season at Bangor, and I was looking forward to it already. There were only seven runners in my race and, although my little grey horse hadn't really shown much on the flat, he'd schooled well, jumping straight and quickly out of my hands on Newmarket Links.

"You're not a number" bellowed out Chris Rea on the cassette player as I drove round the clock tower, too early for the paper shop. I'd have to wait until after riding out my first horse (first lot) before I could see what sort of chance the papers gave me – any price basically. The day was beginning to break through. It was warm already and, as we pulled out, Exning church clock struck 5am.

We hurried through the morning, two quick lots cantering up Hamilton Hill. Then a dash back to Kennett to shower quickly and change into the clothes I'd made ready. Vicky Jones, a trainer's daughter from Oswestry, had left a message on my answerphone and, whilst drying my hair, I got through to her father, Arthur. He told me to leave early as traffic and roadworks were causing long delays. After ringing Jeff Pearce, who also had a runner in my race, I shot back to Exning to pick up David Thom, the trainer of my horse. I was riding on the opening day of the jumps season and that was special for me. As I drove out of Newmarket, with the sun shining brightly, two accompanying trainers totally engrossed in racing papers and fellow jockey Philip McEntee almost asleep, I daydreamed what it would feel like to ride a winner on the first day. It was 11.15am and the four-hour or so drive that lay ahead was all part of the day's work. My only worry was that we would not arrive in good time.

I had ridden at Bangor once before, finishing third in a bumper (a National Hunt flat race), and always liked to walk the course. I was an amateur but when riding with professionals there is no second chance, as I had already learned. Being a female in a male dominated world meant double trouble if you were to accidentally hinder them by any incompetence. You can smile sweetly in the weighing room but it won't wash during or after a race, when jockeys and trainers can be seen at twenty paces, ready to give you the biggest rollicking ever. Fortunately for me I had never crossed paths with any of the pros.

We arrived in plenty of time and the four of us walked the course. The ground was firm but there didn't appear to be too much jar. It was a beautiful summer's day – but there would be no chance to sunbathe; it was time to change into my colours and breeches. I paused for a few moments outside the weighing room to see the winner of the first race being applauded in the winner's enclosure. I hadn't worn these particular breeches before, but had decided to wear them this season for jumping. As I pulled on my newly polished boots, I decided that these bigger breeches were just right for today's job, and they also bore the initials TC in the back! They used to belong to my ex-fiancé.

"Ready Sharr." My valet, Pat Taylor, was ready for me to weigh out. I wished Diana Jones luck as she passed me on her way out to ride in the Handicap Hurdle. We were quite friendly even though we only ever met at the races.

"Looking well, Sharr. Have you been away on holiday?"

"You must be joking, Pat, this colour is from the back garden." He fixed elastic bands onto my cuffs to keep the colours neat and tidy. "Riding for Henry tomorrow then? Will it win again?"

"He should be in the three, but the race is a bit better than the one he won." I sat on the scales.

"Light today Sharr, I'll just go and get some more lead. Somebody's not feeding you at home."

"Nobody's at home, Pat." We chuckled…

I helped David Thom to saddle *Independent Air*, otherwise known as "*The Grey Job*" (nearly all racehorses have nicknames). He looked well and fit, mane plaited and hooves oiled. I gave the girth another tug, and returned to the weighing room leaving David to sponge out the grey's mouth with some water. Diana finished second and was delighted with her horse's first run of the season. "How will yours go?" she inquired as I tucked in my body protector and put my skull cap on, giving my blue shaded goggles a rub over without having to think about it. Getting changed is a sort of ritual, all part of the ride. Everything has to be placed just so, even down to the safety pin that holds the small collar of the colours together. "He's schooled really well and will get the trip. I hope he runs well – all the owners are here."

"Jockeys! five minutes." And I was ready waiting – no premonition, no gut feeling, no worries. I knew I could give this horse a good ride, I had to please the owners to keep the ride. I had a job to do that required 110 per cent and I loved my work. It meant a lot to me to get things right. The male jockeys appeared from the inner sanctum of the weighing room. Steve Smith Eccles, Richard Dunwoody, Graham McCourt. Once I was in awe of them, now I knew I'd never be in the same league but could give my horses, owners and trainers some value and they would never intimidate me.

We walked out into the warm August sun, holding on to its heat with a vengeance. Mum would be home from work, teletext and telephone at the ready. She would never understand why I loved riding over jumps. She'd often stress that Messrs Dunwoody and McCourt were names next to mine in the paper, they were in my race! As if I didn't know. A confident air seems to take over you – the equivalent, I suppose, of a slight high, a buzz. I'd felt it many times but especially now when I was riding so often and people I didn't even know would shout at me from the crowd to "Be Lucky". So many times I looked round at the sound of my name to find the words had come from a complete stranger. That day a boy of seven or eight thrust an autograph book and pen into my black-gloved hand as I reached the paddock. I placed my blue felt-covered whip under my left arm, and although it had happened before (mostly when riding in ladies' races on the flat), I signed my name, blushed in embarrassment at him asking me, thanked him and skipped off into the paddock.

I greeted all the familiar owners and they teased me about the autograph, saying I'd soon be too famous to ride their horses. We laughed as I assured them that was highly unlikely. We commented on how well the runners looked and agreed that I would ride my horse handy and then just see how I went. The bell rang for the jockeys to mount, and I was half way across the paddock thanking them for telling me to "have a good ride". David Thom legged me up onto the grey, who was very much on his toes, and the rest was down to me. I altered my stirrup leathers and then felt good as the grey bounced impatiently underneath me. I patted him down the neck and asked him what he was worried about. He pulled strongly at the reins and I commented to the girl who was leading him how well he felt. She let me go on to the track and he sprang into a strong canter. I locked my body hard against him, trying not to let him get into his stride and, as we neared the start, I was in full control.

The runners gathered in front of the first hurdle, and we assured our novice three-year-olds that there was nothing to worry about. Steve Smith Eccles asked me what I was going to do and I told him I'd be handy but did not want to make the running. He told me to sit with him and we'd help each other over the first couple. This often happens with horses first time over hurdles. "Does that jump straight, Sharron?" The voice behind me belonged to Richard Dunwoody and I answered him "yes", only half turning round. All the girths had been checked and, with a couple of minutes to go before the off (the 5.20 Claiming Three Year Old Hurdle), the boys were saying to each other "not to go mad!", a married man's pace, to start with anyway. We lined up. Steve was on my inner and Dunwoody on my right, ready to drop in behind me as soon as the tapes went up. His horse needed to be covered up in the early stages of the race. I just had time to wipe my eyes under steamed-up goggles, perspiration already rife on me. The starter climbed his rostrum. Then he cried out... "Come on then!"

We thundered towards the first hurdle. My horse was stronger than ever. I challenged Steve for the lead and he shouted at me to go steady. I managed to hold him back; he was not going to get the better of me. Not now. Richard swore angrily, "You said that was straight!" I'd jumped right hand down over the first, my horse acting like he'd never seen a hurdle before. Hence the title novice. Then at the second, "Steve!" I yelled as he jumped right across me. I was pleased with my horse for keeping straight and as we all began to settle down, passing the winning post with a circuit to run, I hoped I looked as stylish as my male counterparts. The thundering of hooves and clattering of hurdles soon disappeared as I quickly began to lose my position, unaware of the faller at the third. The boys had passed me from both sides as we turned away from the stands. Any hope of winning was gone. I urged my grey on just to make sure he wasn't holding back on me. We carried on and, by the third last, were completely tailed off.

Graham McCourt fell at the second last, and horse and jockey were still scrambling to their feet as I approached. We jumped it untidily, and in my mind I knew the grey had done enough. I decided to pull up as I had a good ride at Newmarket the next day. Then, as if feeling guilty and not wanting him to have a last vision of a fallen horse, I decided to pop the last – the owners had travelled a long way and they would probably let me ride him again. Ten out of ten for perseverance. Nought out of ten for self preservation.

There was no sense of falling and no rolling up into a ball like the other times. I lay gasping for air – all this open space and no air to breathe. The sun, still high in the sky, focused cruelly on my face and, as the ambulance man appeared so close, I wondered why. He was taking the air and I could not breathe. He asked me if I was okay. "Yes," I replied, "but I need oxygen." My voice squeaked like Orville, the puppet duck. "I'm only winded. I'll be alright in a minute." It was so hard to speak, my chest was tight and I asked him to give me a minute before I got up. "You must move out of the way of the horse." I asked if the horse was dead. He wasn't. Good, I thought, just winded like me, and I was sorry I'd pushed him to fall. I asked the ambulance man to loosen my body protector, which didn't do wonders for my figure and which at that moment was definitely restricting my breathing. He started to do as I asked but stopped, telling me I wasn't very decent underneath. Meaning I had no bra on! For the first time in my life I didn't really care. I needed more air and I'd started to feel excruciating pains across my shoulders and collarbones. "Oh flipping heck, I might be too sore to ride at Newmarket tomorrow."

They slid the metal stretcher underneath me, and my breathing was eased by the oxygen mask that had replaced my helmet. Then, as they lifted me towards the sky, the man told me to put my legs back on the stretcher. They had rolled off, one to either side. I told him I couldn't move them, I felt too weak. I closed my eyes, taking long, slow, deep breaths. I was annoyed at myself for making the mistake, and hoped these sharp pains would not last too long.

There were lots of concerned faces as I arrived back in the ambulance room. I told everyone I was alright. I muttered something about Newmarket and the doctor said I had to go to hospital. I asked Diana to ring Henry Cecil. Then the doctor was asking me if I could feel my toes, my legs. "Sharron, can you move your arms?" I could hear him clearly and I could see him.

"No, I think I've broken both shoulders and both collarbones." The scream was quite chilling as they removed my body protector. More anxious faces. Brad (Graham Bradley) appeared at the doorway. I smiled and told him I was alright, "just shoulders and collarbones!"

The light sheet that covered me seemed to be causing all the pain. I told the doctor but he assured me my shoulders and collarbones were intact. During the drive to Wrexham hospital I was accompanied by the man who first attended me. I can remember feeling so tired and closed my eyes, drifting into sleep. I don't know if I'd had anything to ease the pain, but I didn't hurt as much. The next few hours remain quite vague. I only remember a few pitiful cries whilst my x-rays were being taken and becoming quite annoyed with a woman who kept asking my name and address, and my mother's telephone number. "I don't want you to bother her," I said. "I'll ring tomorrow when I know I can go home." The woman became quite insistent, saying I was to be transferred to the Orthopaedic in Oswestry and my mother had to be told. It looked as though my stay in hospital would be for more than a few days.

A small dusky man was looking at me as I slid from underneath the scan. He told me he was Dr El Masry. I asked him what the damage was. He was surprised by the bluntness of my question and his face changed from a compassionate smile to a more serious one. "You have broken your neck quite badly."

"But I'm not dead am I?" Another question that made his mouth curl slightly.

"No, at the moment your body is paralysed from the neck down."

"Does that mean I won't ever walk again?"

"How brave are you, Sharron Murgatroyd?"

"I'm pretty brave," I told him, "I'm a Jump Jockey."

He paused for a moment then told me I might never walk again...

August Sun

OoO

August sun... Gaiety and so colourful
For some
Dry heat that burns so gently now
On my body so brown
Excited screams and shouts from the crowd
As we race by
But from my own excitement... So suddenly
So quiet
Now on the sunburnt ground
I lie... Motionless
Beloved horse by my side

I cannot breathe... I whisper slow
I'm only winded I hope you know
August sun
One of the many things
I love
Leave your heat from my face
Take your gaiety and summer colours... I have to move
I'm in the next race
I'll be alright I tell the man
Just give me one more minute... If you can
And as I lie motionless
On ground so warm
They lift me gently... To kiss the sky

But I don't realise... And for now... I do not cry...

OoO

Sharron Murgatroyd

CHAPTER TWO

Horses, Ponies, Friends

My mother was not overjoyed when my dad wanted to buy a farmhouse and land on the outskirts of Halifax. But, as we all would learn in later life, she would forsake all for the welfare of her husband and children, even if that meant giving up her own happiness. So Soaper House Farm, Coley Road with all its surrounding countryside became our home and, by the time I had reached three, our second pet had installed itself in our care – the first still a fluffy ball of fur who grew up to be a very handsome Alsatian.

My dad, who had taken my older brother Clive to have a couple of riding lessons, bought a mare called *Misty*. She was for sale due to the closure of the stables. Originally bought for my brother, it was not long before I was being lifted onto her back. A bad asthma allergy soon put an end to Clive's riding, who by now was into football anyway. Endless happy days were spent in that idyllic setting. But in the winter of 1963, the short move from cold farmhouse (still complete with tin bath and lavatory at the end of the garden) to newly built bungalow did not come too soon for my mum who had just presented us with a baby brother, Mark.

The locals were none too happy about the lovely old farm cottages being replaced by modern bungalows and, with my aunt and uncle who now lived in the "next field" as my mum often called it, we were referred to as "the Townies". But attitudes change and it wasn't long before the local farmers were giving my dad and uncle Bernard a hand, probably feeling a bit sorry for the white collar workers who kept getting the tractor stuck at the back of the house! Although my mum never got used to living in the country, with all its field mice, cats, a dog and now another pony (who was mine) we were all really happy kids. We had everything and it never mattered to us that the only shop was two miles up the road. I never realised how lost mum felt.

With my dad working in Bradford, where he had a central heating business, and arriving home late, and my mum just too nervous to saddle up and take me for a ride, my Aunty Angela's sister would often hear a little voice at the end of the phone, "Can we go for a ride, Linda?" Linda came as often as she could and I prayed for the day I would not need any help. I was just too small to saddle up and I tried all the tricks – standing on buckets, standing on the wall, standing on bales of straw. I can't remember the exact age I managed to put the bridle on myself and, not bothering with a saddle, I jumped from the wall and proudly rode into the driveway in front of the house. My mum didn't know whether to laugh or cry.

Anne Hunter, whose dad was the milkman, was to be my best friend.

We lived and breathed ponies. Day rides to Anne's Grandma Robinson were planned for summer holidays. We would start our journey in the morning, riding from Coley to Causeway Foot and up the road over roundabouts and through traffic lights. We made our way up through Queensbury, then out onto the long country road known as Soil Hill. We would stop somewhere on a wide verge to rest the ponies and to tuck into our picnic, quenching our thirst on home-made ginger beer. At one time I must have had about twenty ginger plants lined up on the kitchen windowsill, until I was told to get rid of them. Easy... I took them to school and sold them. I explained very carefully how they must be split into two every time they were ready, and fed with two spoons of ginger and the same of sugar. So in the end you'd always get your money back, and it was a lovely drink. When we arrived at Grandma Robinson's the ponies went into her paddock. Then, after lunch and a look round the farm, we'd saddle up again and set off home. The round trip was about ten miles; it used to seem more like twenty! Then I suppose for an eight- and eleven-year-old it was quite far enough.

Misty was more like Anne's pony and her first foal, *Prince,* was mine. Unfortunately a second foal suffered a fatal injury and the third (Domino) was sold to another local girl, Ann Binns. The latter was no loss to me. We fell out one winter's night when he jumped at me while I was distributing the hay and I slipped over hitting my head against the black stone wall. Although stitches were not needed, it left a horrible scar and my mum wouldn't let me wear my hair in pig-tails again, and I liked pig-tails. The ponies had a lot to put up with; we'd often jump on them from the wall and they would canter round the field, stopping at exactly the same place. No saddle or bridle were needed on those occasions. We never went to a riding school but we went to all the local shows, shampooing both ponies in Stardrops the night before, wrapping them up in old sheets and hoping they wouldn't get out of the shed in the middle of the field. There were often lots and lots of tears, mostly mine, when an escapee was found rolling in as much mud as he could find.

I pleaded with my parents not to make me go to church on one particular Sunday morning, as *Prince* would have to be bathed thoroughly before making an appearance anywhere. They made no allowances on this occasion and I sobbed all the way there and back wondering why God was so important. I was still being punished for an incident earlier in the week. After realising we had run out of a block of white chalk, used for rubbing on the ponies' legs, I told Anne not to worry. I knew just the right thing to use. Moments later I was dabbing *Prince* with a fluffy blue puff and sweet smelling white powder. Just the job! Unfortunately, when my mum came home and found her bowl of Avon talcum powder called Wishing, lid off, full of horse hair, and blue powder puff a sort of dirty grey colour, she was not a happy lady!

My tears dried when I saw that my two friends, Anne and Elaine, had washed all traces of mud off my nearly all white pony (just a brown patch over one side of his face, chest and a small patch on his tummy) and had left him tied to the washing line! Jodhpurs and jacket were soon pulled on and I went in pursuit, now dreaming of winning rosettes. *Prince*, however, seemed to want to make me the most unhappy child at shows. He would jump anything at home but as soon as I rode him into a coloured jump in the show ring he'd down tools, pretending he couldn't jump. I won quite a few rosettes in gymkhanas but never in the jumping! Later, although it was not my first intention, I was to sell *Prince* – an action I would regret.

The school holidays were looked forward to with relish and our next major event began to materialise. Anne and I had decided to hold our own pony show. It would be held in the field across the road from my house. The beginning of the summer holidays were filled with the organisation of our very own show. With a little help from friends there were jumps to be made and painted, a showjumping and gymkhana ring to be marked out, rosettes to be ordered, schedule to plan, judges to find and our mums roped in to provide refreshments. Anne's dad's pig trailer would do as secretary's tent and we became really ambitious when we decided to have a cross-country course skirting the edge of the ten acre field. It pleased me enormously when the course was finished, as *Prince* jumped superbly on his home territory! Unfortunately, this caused a minor fall-out between us friends when it came to light that I had been "testing" the jumps in the evenings after everyone had gone home. I was banned from the cross-country! I would have an unfair advantage, according to the others... "So what's wrong with that?" I argued, knowing that my time round the course was good and that the winning rosette was almost certain to be mine. However, we did introduce a class for coloured ponies (black/brown and white only) which was unknown at the time. As there were only four that we knew of in the locality, we were odds on to win a cherished rosette – we had two of them!...

August 30th 1970 was a bright and sunny day, and two very excited young girls met to make the last minute arrangements. As it turned out there were no worries or mishaps, and the whole day was splendid. Rosettes won, for us, became secondary to the success of the day. As we counted out the grand total of five pounds profit, which we donated to Bleak Holt Home for Elderly Horses, we were proud of our achievement.

But family life had changed dramatically. My dad had left home the Sunday before the pony show, feeling he loved another women more than his wife and four children – the youngest, Justine only three and a half. So, after persuading my mum that the country was the place to be, he moved out... We stayed at Soaper House Farm until 1972. During this time I continually pushed away the absence of my dad, focusing all my attention on my still eventful young life.

The Annual Show had been on our minds for weeks. Anne and I had saved pocket money so we could enter various classes, starting with the fancy dress. Anne had teamed up with one of the other girls but I wasn't too bothered about that. I had two ponies to ride apart from *Prince*, who was only ever entered in gymkhanas. After the fancy dress I changed quickly onto a pony called *Rusty*. It was his first show and I rode him round for another friend, Danuta, his owner. I knew him well and had ridden him away when first broken in. Today he was being very awkward and almost immediately slipped over. I kept hold of him and was promptly put back in the saddle, but I was quickly taken off again when it became apparent I was hurt. The journey to Halifax Infirmary with one of the girl's parents seemed to take hours. I was eleven years old and had broken my left ankle. My foot hung to the left at the end of my leg, appearing to be a lot worse than it actually was, and I was allowed home when my mum came to collect me. I remained in plaster up to my thigh for six weeks. By the fifth week I was managing to get back on *Prince* and ride him round the field, plaster leg sticking out. I don't know if my mum ever found out about that, but she went mad when she saw me riding on the back of a trials bike with one of my brother's mates. Through this time my mother coped admirably.

Our dad was never going to come home to be a good husband and father, so my mum had to do what she thought was best. We had to leave our friends, our green fields and our pets. My new pony, *Calypso*, was still unbroken. I had wanted to part exchange *Misty* for him, but when I saw how upset Anne was, I let *Prince* go instead. Anne promised to look after *Calypso* so I need not worry. My cat Tigger would often be seen sitting on the wall of our empty house. I'd carried her to Grandma Jackson's, who lived a few yards away, and she gave Tigger a good home. My brother's Alsatian was also found a good local home.

There were no tantrums that I can remember, just repeated questions "WHY?" followed by a lot of tears. The goodbyes were kept brief and, once everything was packed up, we were ready to leave. Our destination was 5 Lynthorne Road, Frizinghall, on the outskirts of Bradford City Centre, where we were to live with my granddad. The cobbled streets and back alleys were now our play areas. My mother, returning to the home that she'd lived in since a teenager and knew so well, found a strength from somewhere to cope, and we did too. Soon Coley Road and days with our mum and dad together would be just a memory.

After having made Lieutenant-Colonel in the army and bringing up a large family of his own, my granddad Conroy tried hard to put up with four very lively kids, but peace and quiet were more on his agenda. After only four months we moved to the other side of Bradford. The council estate at

Rowantree Drive was quite smart compared to most and we soon made friends with the Haste family who lived next door. There were three brothers and three sisters. Janet Haste was a year or two older than me and we became good friends. The most disappointing thing about the move was another change of school. I had already been to two secondary schools and I wasn't thirteen yet. I hated my new school, St Georges, and any excuse not to go was taken. My mum would often see me onto the bus but, instead of getting off at school, I'd carry on into town. Sometimes, if money was available, another bus from the Exchange would take me back to an old familiar place. I missed my pony and the fields desperately, and now I had to look after my younger brother and sister at weekends so my mum could work. My trips to Coley were becoming fewer and I was having to grow up fast. I would often be left enough money for a pound of mincemeat or stewing steak and would make the stew for tea. Sometimes, though, I only bought half a pound of stewing steak and with the change I bought five Park Drive cigarettes! I would use more vegetables then but was nearly found out once. After Mark, Justine and myself had eaten, there were only a few pieces left, which I ate while I was re-heating it for my older brother, Clive. He complained to my mum that there was no meat in his stew and she told me off for only giving him vegetables. I bought the full pound after that. Janet and I were allowed to go to the Mecca dance hall for the under fourteens but we always used to go on the Tuesday to the over fourteens, which was much more fun...

Calypso needed riding – he was fast becoming a good sort. I showed him in-hand, which means I led him round the show ring, and he came third. But my dream of the new style pale yellow jodhpurs, blue riding jacket with velvet collar, and him kitted out with matching browband and plaited blue reins never came true. It became evident he was not getting the attention he needed and now, quite well schooled, I sold him to a riding school in Rawdon. I held the slight profit in my hand and, although we would end up moving not far away from the riding school, I never saw him again. I went to Coley only a couple of times after that and rode at a few shows but, at the end of the day, if you didn't have your own pony you were left like a spare part. The others didn't like me winning rosettes on their ponies (anything from Handy pony to the showjumping) even when I told them to keep the rosettes. I had found out that a young girl who lived at Clayton Heights owned *Prince* and I went there at weekends for a while to help them ride. But now *Prince* would stand on his head for me, so it was frustrating for them. I hoped I would have my own horse again someday but for the time being my riding days were over.

1974 brought another change of school, to my relief, with my mum getting re-married. We moved to Yeadon and I started going to Benton Park Grammar School, which is where I met Lindsay Beanland. We became good friends after our initial meeting in the gym changing rooms, where it first seemed that we were going to be enemies rather than friends. I often think when a new person starts at a school there is usually somebody ready to have a pop at you. Well, on this occasion it wasn't Lindsay but her friend Janet. Only Janet wanted Lindsay to do the thumping. Janet told me I'd be sorry when Lindsay got hold of me, whereupon I retaliated with a few choice words. The doors of the gym flew open and a gasp from the other girls in my form was followed by Lindsay telling me she wasn't about to thump anyone. "We are a bit old for that sort of thing," I told her without looking up from pulling on a pair of thick blue socks and lacing up my fairly worn out brogues. We were both fourteen and the next two years would find us inseparable. The following year we were in the same form and, even after being at school together all day (or not as the case may be!), most evenings we would sit up in her bedroom, listening to her favourite Rod Stewart or my David Bowie. And when her mother called up the stairs, "I hope you two aren't smoking up there," we both answered in unison "No"... as we chucked the fags out of the window, grinning wickedly at one another.

We went through all the usual teenage stuff – lots of different coloured make-up, all shades of hair colour (from jet black to a deep mahogany red) and the biggest platforms you could possibly walk in without receiving grievous bodily harm. There were many times we walked home from Yeadon Lib. Club with shoes in our hands because our feet were stinging so much. The walk home was not too far, and we both lived on Queensway only about ten doors apart. Lindsay had lived in Yeadon all her life but when we went off anywhere else lots of people thought we were sisters. It was a long walk one Saturday afternoon to the Post House Hotel at Bramhope but someone had told us The Bay City Rollers were staying there whilst they were in concert at Leeds. The world and his wife had tickets to go but our source had not come back with the goods. So we decided to go to the hotel, hoping for a glimpse of the popular group. We thought it strange that no one else shared our knowledge as everywhere was quiet and we went in the back door unnoticed. After wandering about for a while a cleaner saw us and, although we tried to act as if we were staying there, it was obvious we were up to no good! We scarpered quick only to find out they were staying at the Dragonara, now the Leeds Hilton; right time, wrong place! Weekend work was the next thing to fund our make-up and discos. Although it was me who liked the outdoor life and the animals, it was Lindsay who got a Saturday job on a farm and I began working at the local supermarket. After a couple of weeks I was promoted to working on the tills. I liked that best.

To say we were "born too late" is an understatement as our schoolgirl crushes were always for the older boys. Mine began at fourteen for Ian French (Frenchy) and lasted, unfortunately for me, until I was seventeen, when he eventually asked me for a date – but he went to the wrong pub and assumed that I had stood him up! Sad but true. Rod Stewart and the metalwork teacher were the only ones Lindsay would admit to but I'm sure that there were others!

After talking very briefly within the family about emigrating to New Zealand or Australia, we got as far as Highfield Terrace, Saltaire. It was still alright for me to get to school and, although it was a long day, I didn't mind. The atmosphere was often fraught at home and all of a sudden the question, "And what are you going to do when you grow up?" was asked. At that time I had no idea. The careers teacher was fast losing patience. We were due to leave school on May 28th 1976. I had scraped two O' levels – English (how, who knows?) and Environmental Studies. The latter achieved by time spent out in the environment! It was now the beginning of April. Everyone else was either staying on or had some sort of job to go to or was a trainee for something or other. Lindsay got work in a wool factory in Yeadon and there were still some vacancies. I knew what I didn't want to do but I didn't know what I wanted to do… I would hear my mum sticking up for me as my step-father shouted that I was just lazy and didn't want to work. One evening after school my mum arranged for me to have an interview at the hairdresser's, which was within walking distance from our house.

"Are you artistic?" the man said.

"I don't think so," I replied. I might as well have stayed at home. He was thinking that – and I knew it…

A couple of weeks later and still jobless, I went to see a chap called Jeff Crossley. He used to organise trips to Southport and Blackpool for all the kids who lived near when we stayed with my granddad. "You like horses, don't you?" he said after asking me if I had a job.

"Yes, but I don't want to work in a riding school and I haven't ridden for over a year."

"What about racehorses?" My face lit up. I remembered when Anne and I were kids seeing a chap on a shiny black thoroughbred from a small stud. We often rode past on our ponies but were turned away because we were too young for a job. A girl Jeff knew had gone into racing. He gave me her mother's number and the rest was up to me. I couldn't wait to go to school on Monday and tell the careers teacher. My mum was a bit shocked when I told her. Where would I go? Would I still be able to live at home? I didn't know the answers to any of these questions, I only knew that this was what I wanted to do. I felt really good. After all, I wasn't being awkward – I just needed the right thing to come along…

Monday morning was greeted with much more life than usual. The careers teacher was quite taken aback with my new found enthusiasm, as I told her what job I wanted to do. She had never had a pupil go into racing but assured me she would do her best to get all the information I would need. Within a couple of days I was busy writing to lots of different trainers up and down the country. Malton, Middleham, Newmarket, and the Apprentice School, then at Goodwood. I was a good eight-and-a-half stone then and the required weight for most was at least a stone lighter. I was turned down as the replies started to come back. I wasn't going to be put off. If I had to lose weight, I would, and started an immediate diet.

I received a letter from a man called Mr Lindley. He had a good friend who trained in Doncaster and there was a job if I wanted it. He'd arrange for digs for me and I could go on Friday May 28th, the day after leaving school, ready to start work on the Monday.

My Prince

OoO

I have pictures of my pony
Pictures on the wall
I have pictures of my pony
Prince
I loved him most of all
I dearly loved my pony
But then he had to go
I was growing and he didn't want to do
All the things - I wanted to
Go to shows and jump a clear
But he refused to move up
A gear
Just gymkhanas that's all he'd do
But at first it wasn't him
That I did mean to sell
After all I'd known him all my life
And he loved me - I could tell
It was his mum called
Misty
It was her to that man I'd send
But there lay a problem
She was loved by my best friend
Anne tried to raise the money
Twenty-five pounds
Was all she had
And in 1972 at only fifteen
That wasn't too bad
But forty pounds I needed
I had it in my head
A golden horse was for me
A flashy sight to see
We'd ride into the shows
New blue jacket with velvet collar
and matching hat on me
And he would have
Blue plaited reins
A velvet brow band
And envied we would be
Plain old Prince was brown and white
Not shining like before
When I had won my first rosette
And sat on him at four
He didn't want to go into the horsebox
That came to take him away
And if he could have talked

16

He would have cried "let me stay"
My brother and sister watched
Hoping he would not go
And my mum what to do she did not know
At last he went into the horsebox
The Palomino was handed to me
I held some money in my hand
But cried for my Prince - To be
Home again in Coley road
With his mum and with me
The man drove him away
His screams stayed in my dreams
And Misty I could see was sad
And she kept away from me
I was already twelve she said
how would it be
"If someone took you away
And your mum never again
You would see"
I called the colt - Golden Calypso
Even though an ugly duckling was he
I led him round wondering where Prince would be
My friends were very quiet
Mark and Justine hated me
And my mum she was upset
Because my dad wasn't there to guide me
And even though my dream never did come true
of riding Calypso at a show
He did grow up to be flashy
And I sold him for a lot more
But most important at the end
I found my Prince again
He was owned by another young girl
And I used to go and help them
My Prince he always loved me
Even though I sold him short
He had a friend called Sandy
And saw Misty at the shows
And I hope he did forgive me
When I sold him - in Coley Road
I lost my Prince when he was sold again
Never to be seen
And I hope he did not hate me
I was only twelve - You see

OoO

Sharron Murgatroyd

CHAPTER THREE

Red Hot Summer

I boarded the train in Bradford the next day. My mother was heartbroken although I never realised at the time. One minute I was there, the next I was gone. She gave me some money to help me along; it was only a few pounds as things were not good. That didn't matter to me, I assured her, I'd be alright. It felt that I'd been grown up for a long time. I could cook, clean and look after children, and none of these things I would miss. It was a tremendous feeling to be free…

I had to learn everything at Bob Ward's yard in Doncaster, and my first day was nearly my last. I was lodging about eight miles away with Doug and Barbara Brown at Armthorpe – their son Steve worked for Mr Ward in his school holidays. We biked to work, setting off about 6am but, when Steve realised how slow I was, he told me that I had better set off about 5am… He thought I'd slipped him once but I got carried away with the beautiful morning, cycling along the country roads and singing at the top of my voice, and I missed the turn and ended up in Bentley miles from where I should have been in Askern.

I soon learnt that you do not make too many mistakes in racing. You're on your own and you soon learn to be tough. I had an eventful two months at Mr Ward's and if that didn't put me off then nothing would. "Can you ride work?" David Wilkinson said, on my first day (he was in charge of all three staff, which included his girlfriend Carol, Steve and now me).

"Yes," I replied, not really knowing that "work" meant riding at a gallop. I also forgot to mention to him that I'd never ridden a thoroughbred before.

Steve helped me tack up a three-year-old chestnut filly, *Emmies Gem*. She was what is known as a "right cow". She made no allowances for my inexperience. After the first canter, which we negotiated well, she went flat out when I turned her round for the second. Mr Ward stood precariously waving his arms at the gate. *Emmy* knew where to stop and I had never been so fast on horseback in all my life. I remember wondering if you got quite the same feeling when you were in control! I managed to stay on board that time but it was not long before I'd hit the deck…

It wasn't very long either before I would become attached to a four-year-old colt, *Basalt*. Bob Ward used to call him the quietest colt in England. However, after six weeks of box rest he decided that rearing was the thing to do, especially when I started to ride him. He would go so far down the road, stop and rear so high that sometimes my stirrup leathers came out. He would then turn towards home and jog back pulling hard. I thought my arms would break... Why does everyone, including horses, take the mickey?

I had a few falls. One off *Emmies*, after which I was concussed and only really came to after riding out my second lot. I'd been dying to ride a two-year-old, *Yandina*, then when I did I couldn't remember due to being concussed.

My two months in Doncaster seemed to be longer. For the last two weeks I had been staying with Mr Ward, his wife and two young sons Ian and Jason, whilst Doug and Barbara Brown were on holiday with Steve and David. With only eight horses now and four staff Mr Ward could not keep me on, even though I didn't want to leave. I told him I'd had an interview date to see a trainer called Tony Dickinson but in the meantime Mr Ward had taken me on, so I'd rung Mr Dickinson to tell him I was fixed up. Anyway by the sounds of it he seemed to want someone experienced and not really a school leaver. "Tony Dickinson!..." exclaimed Bob, and with that promptly rang up Ribblesdale Stables. I could go and see the Dickinsons the next week for an interview. I didn't have much packing to do and by the weekend I was back home in Shipley. But now, with a taste of something so very different, if I didn't get the job at Dickinsons I knew I'd get a job somewhere else in racing. I wanted to work and I wanted to be with racehorses and it would not matter where. I would have gone to the end of the earth if necessary. Luckily I didn't have to travel quite that far.

Tony Dickinson told me to come on the Tuesday. "Have you got anyone to bring you?" he inquired.

"No, I thought I'd come on the train," I told him when we spoke on the Sunday. I'd have a job on, Gisburn had no train station, he said. There must be a bus then, I would find out and ring back to confirm a time. After finding out all the bus times, I still needed a lift to Skipton bus station. My mum was working but could take me. We set off very early and I remember sitting in her little blue mini van having a quick cup of coffee out of a flask she'd made for me. I would not take it, I told her, and she was concerned that I had another hour to wait before my bus left for Gisburn. She had to go so as not to be late for work. It was a lovely warm day and in no time at all I was stepping off the bus and asking a chap where Mr Dickinson trained.

I remember clearly wearing a pair of smart green flares, a light fawn mottled jacket and platforms. "I really would like to see you ride out," Mr Dickinson said. From feeling really smart and grown up (remembering he wasn't too keen on taking on youngsters) I then felt quite stupid. I hadn't come properly prepared. Luckily we were still in the days of the jeans and welly brigade, and I was soon handed a pair of wellies and a horrid yellow helmet with a black plastic peak. I was legged up onto a light chestnut among sniggers of unseen stable lads coming out with the usual comments, "Oh, here's another one for us to sort out."

Robert Earnshaw, in only his second year with the Dickinsons, was sent out with me for a walk and trot round the roads and, apart from asking too many questions and generally talking too much, I was okay. The morning went quite well for me with no hiccups. Mr Dickinson would give me a ring later on in the week and was I alright getting back home? I was... All buses connected on the way back to Shipley but I would have happily stayed and started work that very minute. I had done my best; now all I had to do was wait and hope...

I was so enthusiastic and excited when I got home, telling my mum what a lovely place it was and how many horses were there, that she cautioned me not to build up my hopes too much. The next day Tony Dickinson rang to say I could start on Monday. He would take me on one month's trial...

I started to sort out my room, throwing lots of old stuff out, lots of junk. I wouldn't be needing any of it any more. My mum took me all the way to Gisburn, assuring me I only had to pick up the phone if I did not like it, or if it turned out to be too much hard work. She never had such a phone call. I learned so much in the next three and a half years. You never really appreciate things at the time but when I look back I realise how lucky I was to be associated with good horses and such lovely people.

CHAPTER FOUR

Working for the Dickinsons

The first horse I looked after was a gelding called *Pat Hand*. He had run on the flat and was now to be tried over jumps. He was owned by the Haggas family who had quite a few jumpers and also flat horses with Jeremy Hindley. The Gisburn estate was owned by the Hindleys and Ribblesdale stables occupied a small part. It was set out well in four separate yards. The garden yard was my favourite where the horses looked out over Mrs D's well kept lawn bordered with flower beds. The feed house yard was tucked away at the back and the tack (saddle) room yard only had five boxes and was horrid to sweep as it was cobbled. The main piece was named after one of the horses, *Town Head*. This was easy to sweep but was always split in two: Town Head up and Town Head down.

I soon settled in and one of the girls, Sue Goulder (now Bowker), was in digs with me. We became good friends, as I did with the only other girl, Yvonne Johnson (now Redhead). They helped me a lot and were brilliant at their job. They could ride any of the horses and were often on the odd one or two that could be difficult. I had a lot to learn and a lot to live up to. But then, if you didn't learn there you wouldn't learn anywhere... By the end of the month I was doing most things the right way, which was their way. Whether from the way you left your tack hanging up or the way you swept the yards, you took pride in your work and we all loved our horses. The only real arguments were if someone had left one of the horses without a rug on or uncomfortable in any way. My riding needed improving and I was only riding walking and trotting. I did my horses well and I must have shown I was not afraid of hard work. At the end of my first month the boys started to wind me up. "Murgy, write and tell us what the new job's like," one would say. "That's if you get one," another would retort. I knew they were winding me up but I was still worried. Anyway, the Boss, being the gentleman that he was, soon put me out of my misery, so to speak. "Do you want to stay then?" he asked casually as he felt *Pat Hand*'s legs, making me feel as if I was doing him a favour.

"Yes please, if that's alright."

"I don't usually have young uns," he was half way out of the door, "but you're not a bad lass and you try hard." He was already in the next stable.

"Does that mean I can stay?" I called through to the other side of the wooden stable.

"Yes, you can stay." I hugged *Pat Hand* round the neck, I was so happy, and he laid his ears back and tried to bite the wall – he didn't like too much fuss.

Later on that day, my name firmly stuck over my tack and the grooming box already with the letter M on it (cleaned and ready for action), I phoned my mum with the good news. I didn't have to wait long to lead in my first winner, *Pat Hand*, at Catterick. I was proud and excited as we stood in the enclosure by the plaque that said "Winner" - it was a special moment and Pat had been ridden by Michael Dickinson, the Boss's son. It was bitterly cold – the lads used to call it Catterick fridge.

It was 1976 and the stable housed a number of stars at that time, but all I could do was stroke them over the door. However, it was not long before being legged up onto one "who knows more than you will ever know" was a regular occurrence. *Dorlesa* and *Donohill* were good rides for me round the roads and, on very special occasions, I was allowed to ride *Winter Rain*, even though he was one of Mrs D's rides. Sadly for all of us he was killed in the '77 Grand National and Mrs D was devastated. *Red Rum* made history with his third Grand National win and, as the nation cheered a hero, we mourned our friend... I never rode *Broncho II* (pronounced second) but the next best thing was *Brother Broncho*. He, unfortunately, was not in the same class but just as hard to break-in. He was the first racehorse I had an affinity with but by no means the last. It can be such a heartbreaking job – sometimes I wish I'd never seen a horse (or a man!). When that special one has to go or is injured, you swear you will never get attached to another. But you always do, you just cannot help yourself, you always do...

We all got on tremendously well at the stables. Living in such a small village we all saw a lot of each other. After work it would be changed and down to the New Inn or Ribblesdale Arms. Pool matches were high on the agenda and, even though late nights were often early mornings, we were never late for work. Time off ill or being late was unheard of at the Dickinsons. Every so often we'd all pile into a couple of cars and go to a good night club in Blackburn – sometimes I'd wonder if we were stuck together. Even when the lads found a girlfriend they seemed to always bring her back to Gisburn. The New Inn was probably our favourite haunt, with the blacksmiths Jacko and Harry Driver and a travelling perfume salesman whose name I can't remember, often providing the entertainment. Anyway, the main point of the exercise was to have fun and no hassle. Yvonne and I would often venture out on our own and I remember our drink of that time was Blue Bols and lemonade. It helped with introductions to the local talent as well when they were curious about what we were drinking!

My first year was spent doing the basics and a lot of walking and trotting. Everyone took their own horses racing but there were occasions when there was a spare. I loved going racing and always volunteered for the spares – anyway, it was getting pretty boring just riding the ones that were walking on the road or leading out the ones that were having an easy day. I wanted to canter although at that time I had no aspirations of wanting to be a jockey, just to canter the ones I looked after. These included *Pat Hand*, who had now won two races, *In Chancery*, who had managed to win one, and *Woodflame*, whose owner decided to move him before he could win anything. There were valid excuses for the latter two, especially *Woodflame* who arrived back at the yard one morning with a bleeding mouth because he had pulled so hard with one of the lads. Mrs D was having none of that. She put it down to bad hands and rode him herself the next day to prove it! She was a marvellous horsewoman, very strict with the way she wanted things doing but that was her prerogative and I respected her for it. I found myself with the same attitude in later years.

Boss thought the horses would just be too strong for me but I was getting restless. I felt as if I was not learning any more. By now most of the horses were being roughed off and turned out to grass for the summer. "There will be plenty of cantering for you next season," Boss said one evening stables and I knew my wait would soon be over because he always kept his word.

These were happy carefree days when the jokes and pranks were taken all in good heart. One Sunday morning three of us girls watched Andrew (Drew) Trotter, who was Scottish, wash, dry and polish with pride his newly acquired red BMW. He then jumped in the works van and drove off in the direction of the telephone box. The chance was too good to miss, and I slipped out armed with talcum powder and liberally doused his pride and joy. He couldn't believe his eyes when he returned and then looked straight up towards our flat window. I opened the window, "Hey, Drew, what's happened to your car? It's covered in white stuff."

"I'll get you for this," he shouted, "I know it was you." By now we were nearly on the floor in hysterics. People were driving past, slowing down to have a look, and Drew didn't know whether to laugh or cry.

"Keep your kilt on, it's going to rain tonight anyway!"

"You're dead, Murgy, when I get my hands on you." He did laugh though, one day about a week later!

There were lots of the horses' rugs to wash and, after they had been brushed down they were soaked in a bath of Jeyes fluid (a very strong disinfectant). We then scrubbed them with hot soapy water and hosed them off. I couldn't resist flicking the lads with a quick spray of water as they walked past and Mrs D chuckled at my cheekiness. I was well safe while she was around. Unfortunately the next minute she hopped in the car and drove away. Drew, Renny and Robert appeared grinning; there was nowhere to run, nowhere to hide. My struggling was in vain, and they dragged me towards the bath with its strong smelling milky looking liquid and I was held there fully clothed until I was soaked to the skin! I smelt of the stuff for a week.

The next few weeks were spent with regular visits to the indoor ride on

In Chancery. A few riding lessons and getting a feel of cantering were just what I needed. My horse was quite wooden-headed at times and the Boss was pleased it settled him down quite a lot. When I told him I'd been jumping him, his smile was broad and caring.

Renny (Graham Rennison, one of the lads I worked with) stuck up for me when, after two months trotting, the jumpers were ready to start steady cantering on a rotavated strip. Neither *Derby Court* nor *Pat Hand* pulled, he told the Boss. I rode *Pat Hand* and never looked back. At last I was trusted, I was capable. It felt wonderful going the same way instead of branching off for a trot on my own. The others would never realise how I felt. *Pat Hand* was bomb proof even when he was quite fresh. My riding improved no end throughout 1977 and riding *In Chancery* round the 37 Acre proved I was capable of riding something stronger. Now I had a new horse to look after, and I wondered if I'd ever be able to ride him.

I started to have driving lessons as soon as I was seventeen, and passed my test, second time, just before I was eighteen, with the help of a local lad called Alan Haythornthwaite. He used to let me drive his car when we went to a nightclub or to the "Trotting Races" at Manchester or Kendal. He still helped me, even when one night I nearly hit a lorry. "Watch out!" he screamed. "Miles away, don't worry," I smiled, but he was white. I suppose I must have been a bit close. Anyway it wasn't long before I'd saved up and bought my own car. One day, before I'd got it insured, I was busy polishing it when Renny came along and said I should be practising changing tyres. My lesson went well and I also found out that the dip stick was not that bloke who went in the pub. Oil and water… check… tyres and petrol… check… It came in handy one morning driving back to work from my mum's. I had a puncture but promptly changed it. The milkman was well impressed.

I'm A Driver (my new horse) would never have set the world alight on looks. We had trouble keeping any flesh over his light, agile frame. Three eggs and a pint of Guinness every night helped but Mrs D had her work cut out making him eat. He was a gentle horse to take care of although, when he first came over from Ireland after winning a bumper, he lacked a bit of character. The Boss was often mad at him; the way he'd stand in his box – hind legs crossed and head down, food still in his manger. A time bomb waiting to explode…

He was a quiet horse in the stable and would nearly go to sleep when I brushed his face at evening stables. But when he was being ridden, even on the roads, he always had to be in front or else he would throw himself about and canter on the spot, sliding on slippery winter roads. Ending the season with two bloodless wins in novice hurdles, we wondered how he would take to fences!

During the summer of '78, whilst the jumpers were out at grass, I did a short stint at Jeremy Hindley's (a trainer in Newmarket). After it I felt a lot more confident. My first morning back at Dickinsons I rode a lovely big horse I looked after called *Tempting Times*. As I was just about to leave the yard with one of the other lads a voice called out, "Just a minute dear." It was Mrs D asking me if I thought I was Lester Piggott, as she lengthened my stirrup leathers. I knew "*Tempting*" could be quite strong so I was riding short, as I had on the flat horses in Newmarket. "I hope you haven't picked up any bad habits, dear, while you've been away," she grinned at me, and I told her I didn't think so. A lot of people think that if a horse is a strong puller then you have to ride with your stirrups shorter to anchor them but Mrs D never rode short and she rode some of the strongest horses in the yard. It was all a matter of settling your horse and not dragging at his mouth. You will often hear people involved with horses saying a rider has good hands or bad. It's like some people are heavy handed. The head lad at Hindley's, Bill Henderson, used to like me riding a filly called *Double Lock*. One day when I asked him about it he said under his breath, "You've got good hands."

"Sorry, Bill, what did you say?"

"Nothing," and he was half way down the yard, not one to give compliments. I was made up!

We were all very excited at the start of the 78/79 season, with a number of new equine inmates and a new jockey. We were waiting to pull out one morning when a new lad appeared from the feed house yard. "He won't last long," we scoffed. He was riding short and carrying a whip! "Wait until Mrs D and Boss see him." Of course, it was us who were left feeling like dorks – rising Irish star jockey, Tommy Carmody, had arrived. This was the way he was and nobody was going to change his style. The horses were getting fit and were quite fresh but Carmody rode everything the same length – short. We all waited in the first few days for him to hit the deck but, even when they turned themselves inside out, Carmody hardly moved. When they had finished messing about he'd give them a pat down the neck explaining to them with a few choice words, usually beginning with F, that they really should behave because he was here to stay! He didn't ride *I'm A Driver* when he first started cantering, that was Brian Powell's (Beano) pleasure. He used to go into the field first so he could trot away quietly but the Driver had other ideas. As soon as he felt grass under his hooves, he would plunge and twist. How he never fell over I don't know and Beano stuck to him like glue.

Beano had had a few rides but didn't ride in races any more and, although he and Carmody were so very different, I admired both. They were always there to help and not take the mickey. When I knew that I wanted to ride after tasting the excitement of galloping and schooling the horses over hurdles, Carmody was the first person I dared to tell.

I rode *I'm A Driver* for all his road work but I also took over a young metallic chestnut. It wasn't often the Boss bought horses off the flat but, with a few turning out quite good, he'd taken a chance on this well made three-year-old who had won at two but, in his words, seemed a bit of a monkey now. *Badsworth Boy* was very cheeky but proved himself no monkey. (He went on to be three times Champion two mile chaser at Cheltenham.) I loved all my three horses and although *Brother Broncho* would never be quite as good as the other two, he taught me a lot and I didn't like anyone else riding him. I was really proud when leading up any of the horses at the races, not just my own. They always looked well and now Mrs D had taught me to plait their manes and Sue had showed me how to plait a tail (which is not easy) a Dickinson horse nearly always won the best turned out in their race.

My first taste of schooling a racehorse had come when Boss and Mrs D were on their annual holiday, three days in the Lake District... I think at that time Bud or MD (Michael Dickinson) could only be let loose with running the yard for those few days. Anyway, we were hacking round a straw field when Bud decided to jump over a few bales. "You first, Murg," he called to me. I was on a handicap hurdler called *Waite* who never quite took to fences and was about the only handicap hurdler we had. I pointed *Waite* in the right direction and he basically did the rest. It was wonderful. Michael would always fill us with lots of confidence. Sometimes Boss would think a particular horse he had put me on would be too strong. "D'yea think yea can hold that?", Boss would say and Michael would chirp in, "Course she can... Now you won't let me down, Sharr!" I was stretched to my limits but I never let him down and it became a challenge. In fact everything did... I wanted to be the best at everything I did.

After schooling *Waite* under Michael's supervision my riding seemed to improve every day. I was trusted to ride many stable stars. I did not mind riding one down the road when it was a smart hurdler, like *French Hollow* or *Silver Buck* – who went on to win the Gold Cup.

Now instead of changing over horses with the lads at the jump field, I was getting a chance to do some schooling. I didn't mind changing over when it was Tommy, Robert, Brian or Michael because you could always learn something by watching them, especially when Boss pointed out good and bad things. But it used to annoy me when I'd see one of the younger boys, whose tack had virtually fallen off the day before because his girths had not been tight enough, stride over and jock me off.

Over the next few months I enjoyed riding a lot of galloping and schooling, often riding a variety of horses in the yard. I rode *Badsworth Boy* in his first piece of work and afterwards wrote on the gallop report that he "never came off the bridle". We all had to write down on a pad how our horses had galloped, if they had become very tired, then it could be referred to the next week. I'd finished just behind three of the other lads but I hadn't moved. That was my first real feel of controlled power and I was on a high. It didn't feel as good as that first day at Bob Ward's, it felt better! My gallop report read: "Went well, wind good, finished on bridle." I was accused by one of the lads in the same gallop of not knowing what I was on about but when *Badsworth* galloped again, this time ridden by Beano, his gallop report simply read: "Pissed Up!!"

I rode *I'm A Driver* over to the schooling field with *Cavity Hunter* and Tommy Carmody. Michael was supposed to be meeting us at the gate, but as we trotted towards the bottom field, Boss pulled up in the car and there was no sign of Michael. "You better just walk up," Boss told us. Tommy insisted I'd be able to canter my horse and at last I was going to canter the strongest puller in the yard. Boss had visions of me disappearing over the horizon, but *Driver* never even took hold of the bridle. He seemed to know not to pull too hard and I thought now I'd be able to ride him every day. Ten minutes later he and Tommy were heading for a line of three schooling fences at 150 miles an hour!! Tommy had earlier scoffed, "He'll soon slow down when he sees a big fence coming towards him." Needless to say he did not...

I'm A Driver won at Ayr first time out, putting in a fine jumping display, unlike *Night Nurse* who had come to grief at Market Rasen. They were both entered in the Bobby Renton Novice Chase and it was heralded "The Novice Chase" this side of Cheltenham. He had only run four days earlier at Ayr and conceded 4lb to *Night Nurse*. The former Champion Hurdler looked in danger of being thrashed at half way but, under a superb ride from Ian Watkinson (who Carmody had been warned had nerves of steel), managed to lead on the run in and win by a couple of lengths. I felt *Driver* was a bit flat that day, feeling the effects from his last run, but they never met again. This was mostly due to the ground and the stepping up in distance for *Night Nurse*.

We soon found another rival to take on *Night Nurse* – yet another winning debutante, *Silver Buck*. With a more controlled way of racing, neither *Night Nurse*'s greatness nor Watkinson's nerves of steel were a match for the slightly quirky white-eyed Buck and the flat race precision of Carmody.

The Buchanan Whisky Gold Cup at Ascot was mapped out next for *Driver*, and in it he was again due to meet *Night Nurse*. *Driver* was a hundred and ten per cent – I'd never known him better. He was even getting quite cheeky... Boss and Mrs D had brought him to a peak. The firm ground made *Night Nurse* cry off but *Driver* still had Irish challenger *Jack of Trumps* to contend with, and the unbeaten *Carrigeen Hill*, winner of nine consecutive races that season. It was probably the hardest lead up I ever had in my life. He was soon sweating even though it was a cold November day. Boss asked me twice if I wanted him to take over but I could manage.

Driver didn't know which leg to stand on when Tommy was being legged up and the Boss was now saying that he thought the silly horse had thrown the race away before the start. My heart was in my mouth as he went into a clear lead, flicking over the fences as if they were hurdles. "He won't keep this gallop up," said one of the travelling head lads. But *Driver* jumped the last a long way clear and the cheer from the crowd in appreciation of his performance made me so proud, so very proud. I led him into the winner's enclosure. He stood with ears pricked for the photographs, while the press were anxious to know where he was going to run next – especially when it was announced he had smashed the two mile course record by clipping 1.3 seconds off *Crisp*'s 1971 record time of 3 mins 49.7. "Driver Was Speeding" read one headline; he'd been quicker to cover the two miles over fences than "*Gently Does It*" had been over hurdles!

Talk of the Cheltenham Festival was high on the agenda even though the winter had only just set in. Gisburn was like fairytale land, white over the fields as far as the eye could see. But it wasn't much of a fairytale for us trying so desperately to stop our stable stars slipping on icy roads. The run up to Christmas was a crucial time. We could not allow the horses to get too stuffy as February was always the nightmare month. Luckily there was plenty of snow for us to hack about on. Walking through the drifting snow used to make them work really hard, too. As for us, we just hoped the old coal burning stove in the saddle room had not gone out. The tears would often roll down freezing cheeks. No way could we keep our hands and feet even nearly cold, they were always freezing! Then after the numbing cold, there were the inevitable hot aches when the circulation starts to bring warming blood back to the fingers and toes just before frostbite sets in! Painful…

Trips to the beach at Blackpool were quite good fun at first. We would never know how the horses were going to react to the sand and the sea; some of them loved it and some of them were beggars! The first time there with Michael at the helm we cantered for what seemed like hours. Usually the horses would be fresh and always took hold the first few times, and when you woke up the next day your body ached in places you never knew you had. We went when the tide was out. That worked out about 8am and then about 2pm. So it was two box loads twice a day until the weather broke. We had to wear t-shirts and jumpers under waterproofs because you sweat from the inside and get wet from the outside. The horses liked to wade out in the sea but we were always wary of the channels. On more than one occasion a horse and rider would disappear for a few seconds and the rest of us would roar with laughter. *Brother Broncho* was a great ride and liked going, as did *Badsworth*, and I enjoyed riding them, even when *Broncho* and I parted company one day! Some of the horses who didn't move too well were always better after a trip to the beach. We used to rub them down as much as we could, then rug them up and they would wait in the horse box while we grabbed a hot bacon sandwich from a little cafe near the seafront.

Badsworth Boy never worried about anything. He was a bit of a thug in the early days. He protested about having to stand in the horse box, in a lay-by on Boxing Day afternoon after winning by twenty lengths under Robert Earnshaw. Boss had pulled over for better reception on the radio, so we could hear *Gay Spartan* and *Royal Mail* having a battle over the last few fences. *Badsworth* stamped and shook his head, neighing loudly, annoyed that our attention was suddenly focused on something else. He was promptly told to shut up and I had to stand with him so we could hear *Gay Spartan* power to victory in the King George VI Chase at Kempton Park. It was one of those magic racing days.

I was to experience lots of those days. "Working" on Christmas Day, missing parties and Sunday dinners at home were all made worthwhile by the sheer emotion felt when our beloved horses won.

By February 1979 *Badsworth Boy* was vying for Triumph Hurdle favouritism, and Robert was upset because Tommy had decided to ride him instead of Irish hope, *Slaney Idol*. But not as upset as I was. I wanted to ride in races, I just wanted a chance. Boss wouldn't hear of it. "Girls don't ride over jumps" – his voice was soft but firm. Lorna Vincent was doing alright, I pointed out to him, but the discussion was closed. I was nineteen and knew that time waits for no one. *Driver*, *Broncho* and *Badsworth* would soon forgive me and forget me. I'd planned to have another summer in Newmarket, with Jeremy Hindley and after Cheltenham (where *Badsworth* finished third and *Driver* never ran because of the soft ground) I left Dickinsons on the understanding I could return in July, if things didn't work out. Michael gave me two scrapbooks and told me to keep in touch. I only wanted a chance, I told him. It was a very sad day for me and I can never help wondering what might have been because Lorna ended up having a ride for them sometime later.

The boys gave me a good send off. I would certainly miss them, from Chris (Banner) Bell to Robert, Renny, Beano, Chris McSharry and, of course, Drew, not forgetting Tommy Carmody, MD or Ann and Karen. For a moment I wondered if I was doing the right thing. Good job, good horses, good friends and, with talk of moving to Harewood and being even bigger and better, I wondered if I should stay. Like most impatient youngsters I could not wait. I didn't even know what to expect from Newmarket or if I would get what I was looking for but I had a drive in me to do more with my life. I felt confined and needed to spread my wings.

The goodbyes were short and, I suppose, bittersweet. The Dickinsons had taught me a lot and now I seemed to be turning my back on them as I drove out of Gisburn in my Austin Maxi, one suitcase packed with everything I owned in the whole world.

The snow fell thickly and I hoped I was doing the right thing…

CHAPTER FIVE

A Year at Clarehaven

Newmarket was fresh and alive. There is a kind of buzz in the air, so much to see and so much to take in. You can always spot someone new riding out, unsure which gallop is open or whether to trot or not. The heath has its own set of rules. You should always walk past oncoming strings of horses unless otherwise instructed. It was certainly different to what I'd been used to but not necessarily better.

The first thing was to buy some smart jodhpurs and jacket. Not many jeans and wellies down this way, especially now the flat season was imminent. I went back to J. Hindley's and asked him if it would be possible for me to ride in ladies' races. He thought I would be able to get a ladies' permit to ride but he would see how I got on. After all, I still had a lot to learn. I agreed. I'd never ridden a yearling and would not have a clue how fast to go if I was leading in a mile gallop on a flat horse.

After my previous summer, it was not long before I was well settled in, although I was disappointed that Lydia Meadows (now Pearce) and another girl, Jackie Jones, were no longer there. They both rode well and, like me, were trying to find a job where they would be given the chance of rides. Lydia had started with a new trainer in town called Geoff Huffer. I was the only girl there for a while until sisters Sue Vergette (now D'arcy) and Tick (now Sanders) started one Monday morning, shortly followed by a very scatty friend called Liz. We all got on quite well but I know I used to bore them to death talking about *I'm A Driver* and *Badsworth Boy*, as much as they annoyed me by rubbing in how many rides they had point-to-pointing at the weekend. Sue and I were often paired up together to ride work or go through the starting stalls. Part of the flat horses' training is to get them accustomed to going through the starting stalls which they encounter at the racecourse. That Sue and I had the job disgusted many of the older stable lads, who could often be heard muttering, "Bloody women". Sue and I would have a giggle to ourselves – they had had their chance, now it was our turn!

I had never been keen on doing fillies but, as often happens in big flat racing yards, it is always preferred that girls do them. One of the lads left and I came in for two of his fillies. Down in the bottom yard I looked through the bars on the indoor boxes. *Highland Light*, a scruffy-looking home-bred, lifted her head to see who was there and her big loppy ears pricked, intelligently. One of the lads asked me if I had been sent to do her, and I told him she was my new horse. "Good luck, mind she doesn't kick you." She was unclipped, unkempt and very uncooperative – the proverbial "ugly duckling". Then, as the coldness of March and beginning of April began to subside, at last we began to win with rugs and tail strings and all the things that had made her go slightly potty. My name was fixed next to hers on the riding out board... yet another to become attached to. I was especially pleased when my name stayed next to hers with a yellow square by it. That meant we were galloping, riding work! The most important days were work mornings. As the season got more under way a host of jockeys would appear to replace the stable lads, "jocking off" the unfortunate ones. The breakfast room would then be the place to give the jockeys a good airing, a good slagging, "'cause 'e's lost his bottle anyway."

Highland Light was the fastest thing I'd ever sat on. Three of us were told to come four-and-a-half furlongs upsides. On purpose I dwelt a little, holding her back, knowing how strong my filly could be. When we passed *The Governor* supposedly at half speed I was a good half length in front of the other two, hard on the bridle. If I'd moved we would have shot ten lengths clear easy. And if Brian Powell had been on her he would have simply said "Pissed Up!".

Highland Light only won two races as a two-year-old but they were at Sandown and Newmarket. She made all the running and was in the lead all the way both times. At Sandown her argument with one of the stall handlers resulted in her backing up and kicking the starter's land-rover. Fortunately she was alright. That remained her only quirk, the stalls. Joe Gilbert, the second headman, and myself had spent many evening stables enticing her and assuring her that there was nothing to worry about. The initial time at home went desperately wrong – one of the French pupils of that time pulled strongly on her lead rein when she stopped to have a look. A mixture of temperament and nerves resulted in her half rearing and half twisting, leaving Gareth Jones on the floor and *Highland Light* refusing to go anywhere near the stalls. From then on Joe insisted that I was the only one to ride her through the stalls. She trusted me. *Powder and Patch* and *Land and Sea* made up the trio. *Powder and Patch*'s only claim to fame was beating *Mrs Penny* first time out. That was on soft ground and she didn't reproduce that form again all season. As for poor *Land and Sea* (nicknamed *Fish and Chips* by me!), she was merely the Cinderella who never got to the ball.

By mid summer I was riding a lot of work, mostly on lead horses, where pace was the key factor. This was with the help of Tony Kimberley (stable jockey) and work riders Dusty Miller and the late Fred Adrain who would shout instructions for me to "Go on a bit" or "Steady". At evening stables on the nights before work days, some of the lads would sneak into head lad Bill Henderson's office to see what horses they were riding work on the next day. A list was always made out with the person who was riding the horse to the gallop and, in brackets, the person who was going to "jock them off," if any. I didn't believe them when they told me I was down to gallop *Swell Fellow*, an old favourite who could take a right pull. He was by the same sire as *I'm A Driver*, but he was lame in the morning so I never got to ride him.

The night life in Newmarket was pretty repetitious. Week days I would meet Phil McBride in the Horseshoes after work for a game of pool and half a lager, before going home to our flat. This more often than not would result in getting a takeaway on the way home because the game of pool had turned into a match with side bets, and the one half had become three or four. Weekends it was down to the Golden Lion Disco for a dance. I'd met Phil there the year before. My friend Tess and I used to dance all night. Oh, for the days of "Saturday Night Fever"...

All too soon the busy summer was breaking into breezy autumn and the stable stars were being rugged up warm, being saved for next year! The unlucky ones would be sold. Some would find themselves being schooled over hurdles before the end of the month and some would find themselves abroad. I often wonder how they coped with it all. Different language and a different set of rules but horses are tough and resilient and they cope; they have to. The other two-year-old that had looked quite special, apart from *Highland Light* of course, was a very fast colt called *Rollahead*. He had trounced *Highland* up on the gallops before the Cheveley Park Stakes (a notable fillies' race run at Newmarket) but on that occasion she had been ridden by Tony Kimberley and I suspect all was not well.

The long tails (yearlings) were beginning to take up residence and there was lots of mucking out to be done. The next job was lunging the young pretenders, which is the first step towards breaking them in. A long rein is attached to their headpiece and they trot around in circles in both directions. After a few days we introduce them to the saddle and then to a rider. At this stage they are still "babies" but once we start riding them and teaching them they soon learn. I was allowed to lunge and long rein a filly I looked after; she was by *Steel Heart*. It gave me great satisfaction when I finally rode her away. Everything she knew I had taught her. You always start riding yearlings in the conventional riding style then, as they learn more, the stirrup leathers creep shorter and shorter. Then, by the time a gallop and trial ground called the Limekilns is open, most two-year-olds are doing serious work with no sign of a baby tail or breaking bit. All the winter equipment is then oiled and packed away for another year.

The winter passed quickly but it never was half as cold as Gisburn! A new secretary and competent lady rider had joined us and, of course, by now I was wanting to ride in races more than ever. My ambition was fuelled every time I went through the stalls or even rode a canter. But, there was no room for two lady riders. So, after being totally wound up by the lads, I knew it was time for me to have a chat with Mr Hindley about my ladies' permit. He was very sorry but he knew if he ran horses in that type of race his owners would want Franca Vittadini or Elain Mellor to ride. They were the best. There was no point in me staying. I handed in two weeks' notice and, by the end of the week, had got myself a new job in a mixed yard, flat and jumpers. Mr Hindley said he was sorry to see me go but, as I explained, I wanted to ride and was now leaning back towards the jumpers, which I had missed. I'd take my chance somewhere else. He gave me an excellent reference and, nearly a year to the day I had arrived, I left the boys arguing over who was going to look after *Highland Light*. The Vergette girls had already left and Sue was at Mick Ryan's as his lady rider. I wasn't a Vittadini or a Mellor and I realised as a Murgatroyd I would just have to work a little bit harder. This drive is like no other. I couldn't give up... Not now!

CHAPTER SIX

Cheveley Park

Geoff Huffer's yard was at the top of Duchess Drive, out of Newmarket and on the edge of the surrounding villages. It was an excellent location in some ways, for the idyllic countryside and for a quiet walk or a good trotting exercise. Then, on the other hand, when you turned right almost opposite the now famous Dalham Hall Stud, and headed down onto the heath, the older horses and faint-hearted knew that hard work was in store. It was a long trek back after a good work-out. Good for the jumpers but a little arduous for weak two-year-olds.

There was a great staff at the yard, including Lydia who was secretary. My being there, hoping for a few jump rides, would not affect her as she only rode on the flat. Pat Gibson was a very strict but fair head lad and Paul Howling was assistant trainer. There were two yards and I worked in the main yard. The up and coming Bryn Crossley was stable mimic and top apprentice, and Jimmy Black was destined to be in his shadow for the time being. In fact it became apparent that everyone in Newmarket who wanted to ride ended up at Geoff's!

Things were great to start with, as it always is in a new job. I was riding a lot of work and, when one of the girls left, I took over *Sir Michael*, the previous year's Cesarewitch winner. A striking bay horse with a character to match, he floated across the ground; I always thought he would be a top class stayer on the flat but he seemed to lose his way somehow. I led him up at Ascot in an apprentice race with Jimmy Black in the saddle and he won. But we had to wait ages for the outcome as there was an objection by the second to the winner, and a Steward's Inquiry into possible interference between the first two during the race. We kept the race and I was pleased for Jimmy. Geoff didn't think there was much point in me getting a licence to ride over jumps as it was already May and the present jump season was coming to a close. The requirement was five rides in conditional races during your first season. Before I'd taken the job Geoff had said I could have my licence to race ride over jumps and it was sensible to wait for the new season to begin in August. It would also be good to get some more schooling done. I agreed it was the right thing to do and, in the meantime, I'd be riding lots of work and gaining more experience.

Gleaming Wave, a seven-year-old entire (not been castrated), was as black as the ace of spades except for a flash of white down his face. He was the original Jekyll and Hyde horse. In the box he was a kind horse who liked to be stroked and was never colty although his lad, who also travelled the horses, was always blasting me for trusting him too much. "He'll give you such a kick one of these days if you don't tie him up." It was like the devil possessed him, as soon as he stepped outside the stable. Sometimes he wouldn't even go out of the yard but, if you got rough with him, he would rear and buck, and if he happened to get sight or smell of a filly he was worse. John McLaughlin came steaming up the drive on him one day with a filly in front. Her only escape was for the lad to ride her into her stable. We all thought John was letting *Gleaming Wave* go on purpose but he swore he could not stop him. He would often stop on the way to the heath and usually there was only one way to go then, and that was home. Pat put me on him one day and he behaved very well for some unknown reason. From then on he was my ride. Weeks went by and he even went up the all-weather and I let him stride on. Then, one work morning, I was down to take him over to one of the gallops at the racecourse side, but when we unloaded from the horsebox Geoff sent Mick Miller over to jock me off... They say animals and children can make you look silly, well a childish animal is worse! He cantered sweetly to the mile pole but refused point blank to come back up the gallop and ended up trotting back up the walking ground. He was a law unto himself.

In the mid summer I found myself frequently taking horses over to the racecourse and bringing sweaty ones back to wash down and groom. I asked Geoff for the forms to send off for my licence but at the end of August I was still waiting. Time was being wasted yet again and the final straw came when again I wasn't riding work and one of the stud secretaries, who came to ride out now and again, was riding a gallop. I told Pat I might as well find another job. I knew how to do sweaty ones up! Geoff came into the yard after breakfast all apologetic. There had been a mix up with the list and could I pop in the office to fill in my licence? It doesn't take much to keep the dream going; happy again I asked what I was riding and Geoff, smug as ever, said, "*Gleaming Wave* down the town. Oh, and Sharron, pop a pair of blinkers on him, we'll give him a bit work up long hill!"

Geoff was looking at me like Clint Eastwood, "Go on, punk, make my day...". *Gleaming Wave* had refused to walk out of the yard twice that week in blinkers with one of the lads on, and had stopped twice with me since he'd been over to the racecourse.

Pat told me not to get too upset and, if he started rearing, to bring him back in. Even the travelling head lad, George, looked a little sympathetic. I gave *Gleaming Wave* a hug when I put the tack on, and a mint, basically crawling for him to be good. Geoff popped his head round the door. "See you up long hill. Let him stride on strongly, okay?"

"Yes, Geoff," I smiled sweetly. "Will you be waiting at the bend?"

"Yes," and he thought to himself but I won't see you, and I thought, well, you'll have a long wait!

Lydia helped me fill in my licence before lunch and we were looking in the entries for conditional races. At the end of the month there was one at Huntingdon but it didn't suit the few jumpers we had. Geoff came into the office. "The old horse worked well," I said enthusiastically.

"Yes he did," replied Geoff. *Gleaming Wave* had been an angel – it was my turn to be smug!

By the end of November, still without a ride and seemingly not really any closer, I became increasingly fed up. After being told of a new trainer who was moving into town and looking for staff, I rang up and spoke to the head lad. I told Pat that I would not be there when he returned from holiday, because I could start at the new yard on January 1st. "How many times are you going to change jobs?" he asked.

"As many times as it takes." Nothing ventured... Nothing gained... All I wanted to do was work hard and have a few rides.

The next ten years would see to that, when the highs and lows of racing would touch my heart. Very special people close to me could never really understand this. What it is like to have a winner, what it is like to have a loser, what it is like to be let down again and again but still to keep smiling... When you think you've reached a point where all the hard work seems justified, sometimes dreams are easier to live with... But still we keep fighting with an insatiable lust to ride winners, to get it right and the perfect way is to share it with someone who understands. Then we think we are invincible.

CHAPTER SEVEN

Blood, Sweat and Tears
In the Glory Years

Blood and Sweat...

With only a handful of horses and in just his second year of training, Alan Bailey made no rash promises. "I'll do what I can and give you a few rides, but I can't promise to make you a jockey." His voice was sincere. On January 1st 1981 I began working at Wroughton House and was given a skinny, spotty chestnut to do. Nobody liked *Gymer* so it was just as well I came along when I did. The horses were on trotting exercise at that time of year and one of the other girls rode him. It used to make me cringe to see her standing up in the irons swinging off his mouth, his head in the air – him pulling so hard to get away and her pulling so hard trying to stop him, then wondering why he started to sweat after only half an hour. After a few days I suggested we swop as I was riding a nice grey horse that she looked after. She assured me I wouldn't hold one side of him! I told her I'd better learn pretty fast if I was going to ride over jumps. No disrespect to the girls who worked there at that time, good pony riders they might have been, but when it comes to riding a racehorse the difference is quite considerable as I had already found out. I was pleased I got on well with *Gymer* and I hope he was pleased too.

Fred Town was head lad and he too had worked for Tony Dickinson when the Boss trained horses that ran in point-to-points. "Bloody long time ago, we used to just jump five bar gates in them days to school them and, yea, it was bloody cold but we never moaned." And that soon became the trademark, nobody was allowed to moan and the motto was, "If you don't like it, 'eff off home." Alan had known Fred since they were lads. Fred came from Barnoldswick and Alan from Burnley. Two backstreet boys now on the same level as the silverspooners in the sport of kings. No airs and graces, just get stuck in and all pull together and work as a team. The stories they told were quite unbelievable. These stories would usually be remembered on a Saturday morning when we would work through breakfast, finish early and be invited to play pool in Alan's games room. They used to be life-guards on Bournemouth beach in the summer, then, as the season closed and there were no more holidaymakers left to save (rumour has it neither can swim), they told us that they would ring up old Mrs Dingwell saying, "It's Fred and Alan, have you a couple of jobs for us?"

"Sorry dear, I'm fully staffed," she'd reply.

"Well sack two, we'll be back on Monday!" And she did.

It was a fiver to the winner of the game of pool. I won a few times and lost a few times. It helped take the pressure off, being a small yard with very moderate horses. Our best horses at that time were throw-outs from Henry Cecil's but they won and that was the main thing.

By February I was riding *Gymer* on Southfields, a canter over racecourse side, which goes straight down towards the A45 road and back again, running almost parallel but back to back with the Rowley Mile racecourse. I used to trot him on ahead, setting him off with both hands in the neckstrap, fearing that one small tug on his mouth would give him the notion to go as fast as he could. He was very awkward with his head in the air, and very strong – half with nerves, which is often worse for a rider. My arms felt that they were breaking after finishing a couple of canters.

I hoped to ride before the end of the jumps season. However, *Gymer* had only just turned three and the only other one to ride, *Jolliffe's Double*, had not been broken-in long. Neither would run jumping until the new season began in August. Alan wanted me to have an amateur licence because he felt there would be more opportunities for me and I would be able to ride on the flat in ladies' races as well. I wondered if this was yet another fob-off as I would not be eligible until the following year. But Fred assured me, "If he says he'll give you rides then he will." Fred loved to see the girls get on and I often wished my dad could have been as proud of me as Fred was of his daughter, Melody, when she was riding. I decided to wait.

After a summer break, I asked Alan if I could try to settle *Gymer* and bring his head carriage down by fitting him in a pair of draw reins. I'd seen them used to good effect on one of Dickinson's horses. And since he'd done well for his short break I knew he would be even stronger now. He'd already schooled well, albeit slightly out of control, and the steering was alright. It was just the speed that was erratic. Fred, one morning after seeing me turn *Gymer* in a circle to stop him, shouted at me to get that bloody rubber bit off him and, with a worried look, asked if I still had the nerve to school him. "Yes, he's fine, just a bit fresh."

The Links schooling ground in Newmarket is very flat and speed can easily become uncontrollable. We started off with the three baby hurdles and, by the time we approached the first full-sized one, we were what is called in the trade "trapping" (going very fast). He needed no assistance from the saddle and, before Alan and Fred could descend the stand, I returned to my starting point. I was red in the face and needed oxygen but my smile of satisfaction said it all. The plan with the draw reins worked well. In the autumn a much more controlled horse and jockey were seen on the links and even Jeff Pearce, who was riding then, paid me a compliment on how well schooled the horse was when he rode him for a prospective owner. Sadly,

Gymer was sold at the October sales but all the work we'd done together was not in vain. *Gymer* won three races off the bounce round the west country and I hope it was me who gave him the confidence.

The holiday fare to Australia in the New Year was paid for by some very shrewd betting. Phil, who worked at Bruce Hobbs', and buddy Dave Morris (Henry Cecil's) were never far off, and with them being main work riders at their respective stables there were very few winners that went unbacked. Two big bets that stand out in my mind were first time out *Tolmi*, ridden by Edward Hide at Newmarket, and the backing of *Light Cavalry* ante post for the St Leger. One of Cecil's two-year-olds also won that day at about six or seven to one. It was a good time for betting. The worst result was when a horse called *Jam* was clearly beaten in a photograph on the telly, to me and everyone else who watched it – everyone, that is, except the two who had had a few hundred on. Quick as lightning I switched channels for a jump race at Chepstow. The air went blue with all the abuse fired in my direction. "What the 'effing hell are you doing?" they said in unison as they switched back, and I annoyed them even more by saying a blind man could see it was beaten. When the result was announced I whispered, "I told you." And their answer was unrepeatable! Both are training now in Newmarket.

I filled in my forms for an amateur licence. One of the questions is where and when the licence is required for. I asked Alan when he thought my ride would materialise. "You can ride *Jolliffe's Double* at Doncaster's first flat meeting of the season." It was mid February and I wasted no time. I knew I had to be as fit as I could, so that very night saw me pounding the streets and, barring all setbacks, my day would arrive soon.

At last! at last! at last!

My mother came to stay and I warned Alan, "No swearing in front of my mum!" I would have been so embarrassed if she heard him say the "F" word... After riding out a couple of lots I dashed home for a quick change and to pick up my new made-to-measure racing boots. Then, as my mum and I walked from Park Cottages back to Wroughton House, I told her, "At last this is the day I've been waiting for", and I was happy she was with me.

It was an exceptional spring day and, on arriving at Doncaster, I left Jan Bailey to look after mum while I walked the track. Lydia Pearce came with me, then helped with the rest of the procedures. Alan didn't fill me with too many orders but the one thing he did stress was for me to get as close to the inside rail as I could and to stay there, especially up the straight. *Jolliffe* had run over hurdles a week before and, although this flat trip was a little on the short side and there were another twenty-nine runners to contend with, Alan thought our horse could be in the first four. I just hoped he was right.

It felt good walking towards the paddock and I knew my mum would be proud of me. I'd realised my ambition; how lucky I was. I thought about the girls from school – some of them working in factories, some in supermarkets, some now mothers and wives – and the man at the hairdresser's artistically cutting hair. These fleeting thoughts were soon forgotten, dismissed. That life was not for me! This is what I'd worked for and now it was real, all so real.

The race was over in a flash. One moment I was sitting in the stalls over the far side of the track looking at the rise of earth that faced us, feeling sorry as one rider (Brendan Powell) would not be taking part due to broken girths. Then we were running into the straight in a hopeless position and moving off the rails (the unforgivable) for a clearer run and, just as *Jolliffe* begins to get into gear, it's all over bar the shouting. No fairytale start, no first, no winners' enclosure. A smidgen of disappointment, and the desire always to go one better.

Alan politely told my mother to "Go over there while I give your daughter a rollicking." He pointed out where I should have been and "why had I come off the rails?" The slow start didn't help either. I couldn't get any worse... could I?! My second ride was a non-event. I think that's where Hamlet got their idea for the cigar advert. Give up? Never. I finished the year with six rides including two seconds. The first was on *Hiya Judge* at Redcar, where I didn't come off the rails. It was a magic feeling being led into the enclosure. The next time it was on *Jolliffe* and this made me the first season leading lady rider. The dinner and presentation at Woburn Abbey was held to acknowledge the leading lady jockeys in their first, second and third seasons, and also the champion. I held my huge cut-glass trophy with pride but only kept it for a year, my name engraved alongside the former winners. A smaller replica replaced it and would be mine to keep for ever.

Alan had attracted a few more owners and, no sooner had the flat season started than we seemed to be sorting out three-year-olds for the pending jump season. *Jolliffe* and the hard pulling *Double Meaning* were pencilled in for Market Rasen but, with me now being an amateur, they would be ridden by professionals. I would not be able to ride against the pros until I had had more rides. I nearly had three rides at Fakenham on amateur day in the May but, as fortune would have it, none of them got to the races. Martin O'Halloran had already ridden *Jolliffe* and was now his regular pilot when available. The rest were ridden by anyone who could be bothered to come and school them.

Tony Carroll (TC) started riding out once a week and Wednesdays became our schooling morning. I was never resentful of jockeys schooling. We needed their help and I knew I'd get my share of rides. I didn't know if I would like this particular jockey after his condescending opening words to me of "Have you schooled before?" as we cantered to the start of five hurdles on the dirt track at the links. It was a rare occasion when my wit failed me! Afterwards he explained that it could be quite hairy schooling at some places. After a couple of times I decided he was okay and, anyway, the more he rode out the more schooling I could do.

I finished second at Doncaster on *Jolliffe* after he had had a lay off. This satisfied Alan about *Jolliffe's* well being but it ruined his price for Market Rasen the following Saturday. Where he duly won.

After living with Phil McBride for nearly four years it was by mutual agreement that we parted and, in the couple of months running up to Christmas, I traipsed round Newmarket afternoons and evenings looking for a bedsit. Jeff Pearce had bought a house on Lisbon Road but it wouldn't be ready for tenants until January. I moved in as soon as the paint was dry and immediately started looking in estate agent windows to buy a house of my own. I felt relief. There was no emotion or pain at being on my own but I would make up for that in years to come, and in more ways than one.

After a couple of close finishes, *Ramo's Lady* got her just reward. On a cold wet February day in a selling hurdle at Fontwell she managed to be a nose in front at the line under a very hard ride from TC, beating John Francome (Champion Jockey) on one of John Jenkins' horses. It was TC's first winner since shattering a leg in a freak accident at Alan Jarvis' stable nearly two years previously and had not come before time. *Ramo's Lady* was also owned by Terry Ramsden, one of our latest owners.

I was overwhelmed by the mare's gutsy performance and thought that TC's luck would now change. And all of a sudden, after the initial years of working my ears off to have rides, and after eventually finding somewhere to get them, I knew that I would never be a professional jump jockey. I could see how hard it was for someone as talented as TC to survive, so there would be little chance of me making a living. I would be content to remain with my amateur status, enabling me to ride both in ladies' races on the flat and amateur hurdles. Anyway, as things turned out between TC and myself, I was only too happy for him to ride the stable's runners instead of me when he was available. We became engaged on February 14th 1984 and it was the happiest time of my life.

March means only one thing to people who love jump racing and that, of course, is the Cheltenham Festival. The stands were electrified as the Michael Dickinson trained quintet slogged up the Cheltenham hill to become the first five to finish. (Michael had taken over from his father, the Boss.) The Famous Five were home in the blue riband of races, the Gold Cup. It was a training feat that would be too far fetched for even a fictional story. To be a part of the audience was an honour and a wave of emotion surged through everyone as the boys who were responsible for creating such a spectacle became aware of the finishing order. Their hugs and slaps on the back for each other and their gallant steeds was a touching sight for even the hardest of men.

With Cheltenham over and Liverpool to look forward to, our main work at Wroughton House was getting the flat horses ready for their summer campaign. The old horses were usually in full work, as were most of the two-year-olds. My favourite, which I'd broken in and ridden away, was a *Badsworth Boy/Gymer* lookalike called *Jamesmead*. His owner, Mick Channon, who was then playing football for Norwich City, would often call in to see him and another two-year-old called *Mikev*, which he owned in partnership with Kevin Keegan. *Jamesmead* needed more time to strengthen up into his larger frame so, while the lads were off up the gallops playing jockeys on the other two-year-olds, I'd go off somewhere for a leisurely canter and a pick of grass.

Mikev was nervous from the first day he stepped into the yard. Some horses get better and some don't, and unfortunately *Mikev* remained nervous. So much so, in fact, that just as I had finished a canter on the woodchip that runs parallel with the Cambridge Road, he spooked at two other horses and bolted with me. I tried to steer him to avoid the cricket pitch but the steering as well as the brakes were a lost cause. With both hands on the left rein I tried to pull him into a circle and break his stride but the piece of metal in his mouth just slid through and I was fast running out of turf. He somehow negotiated the turn and started heading back down towards the racecourse. Good, I thought, now seeing the long stretch of green lying ahead of me, convinced he would tire before me. *Mikev*, however, was obviously not bolting as blank as I thought. Cocking his jaw and still in full gallop, he suddenly went right-hand-down and the tarmac of the car park sounded ominously underneath his hooves. I knew it could not last very long. The sensation of sliding along when he fell, unable to keep upright as the shiny metal shoes hit the smooth tarmac, did not last long either. Eric Eldin, one of the trainers, and Mr Hopes, the vet, watched in amazement as the colt slid for about ten yards across the car park. Luckily for me, because of the shortness of my stirrup leathers, my leg wasn't trapped underneath him. I escaped with a broken arm and a tap on the head. I repeatedly told everyone, "It doesn't hurt!" *Mikev* escaped unscathed too, apart from being grazed, sore and walking around with tarmac ingrained in his coat for the next three weeks.

I was five weeks in plaster. Most of this time was spent in Wantage with TC, to recuperate. Then two weeks after the plaster came off and after riding out for a week, I rode *Caro Nome* in the Ladies' Derby at Ripon. *Caro Nome* had been bought out of Bruce Hobbs' yard the year before and had already paid for herself by landing a gamble at Thirsk. I was well pleased, especially for her owner, Ted Annetts, who was a lovely man. He would say I could ride his horse even if it would have a better chance in a professional race and Alan would have to point out to him why I was not riding it. There were more opportunities to win prize money in professional races. It would have been no benefit for me to turn pro. I was too heavy at 9 stone for apprentice races where you then claim (take 7 lb off the horses back). I worked hard at my weight for all my riding career. If I had to ride the horse at 9 stone then I liked to weigh 8 stone 9lb. I tried to keep at that weight but I had to diet constantly. Food was often replaced by running in a sweat suit for forty five minutes, mowing lawns or running on the spot in a sun filled greenhouse. Both my sister and I take after a very stocky grandmother, while both wishing we were more like our light and slender mother.

By now I had bought my first home, 53 Field Terrace Road. It was fun painting and decorating, and just going back to my own home and shutting the rest of the world out... I had grown into a private person who liked my own space, wanting only to share it with one other person...

Our lives were busy and work was hard at Wroughton House. As it is with most small yards, the work is more and the money less than in the bigger yards. Newmarket is a hard place for the smaller trainer, when lads can go down the road, do less and get more pay. After being put in charge of the yard when Fred the head lad left, feeling he needed a change, it was my job to do the feeding, tend to the veterinary side of things and generally keep the yard running as smoothly as possible. I would feed at 6am and, on those dark mornings, I would have to bang the boiler room door with my boot to make sure the odd rat had scurried off. Peter Bloomfield, who had joined us as stable jockey after riding a few winners for us, was a great help even though he was still an apprentice. Alan became renowned for giving apprentices rides, with Allan McKay, Simon Whitworth and Conrad Allen all just about starting out there.

One Sunday afternoon Peter and I came in for a right rollicking because Alan had left instructions for us to ride a piece of work on *Hiya Judge*, which I rode out most days, and a three-year-old. Peter and Dale McKeown were tacking up when I arrived and, as it would be very warm in an hour or so, it seemed logical for them to ride out while I saw to the rest of the things in the yard. When Alan asked me how "*Judgy*" had worked and I told him Dale had ridden him, he flipped. "I wanted you to ride him," he yelled at me. I'd never seen him so mad. Then it was over with.

I wasn't very happy when Alan got the late Arthur (Fiddler) Goodwill in to feed but we were busy and I was needed to go racing as well. I respected the man a lot but the very small portions he served up in no way tallied with the amount of work the horses were doing and, after feeding them myself for the past few months, I knew to a near handful how much all of them would eat. The lads often thought I was being too fussy when I tossed an extra handful of oats into a bucket or sometimes took the same amount out. They would laugh, saying that would make no difference. I knew in the mornings when I gave them their first feed of the day – if they had a bit of a dirty manger, not licked clean, they had had sufficient. I fed every one of them as an individual, like Mrs Dickinson had told me when I was at Gisburn. Imagine my horror when I went into the feed house for feeds for a jumper, a two-year-old and *Hiya Judge*, saw the buckets all laid out and was told to take any three…

My first outside ride came in, of all races, the prestigious Ladies' Diamond race at Ascot where the winning rider receives a diamond necklace. Only by chance when trainer Jimmy Harris rang for Lydia Pearce, who was riding for Mick Ryan, did Mr Ryan mention me. It was a fantastic feeling riding on a such a big race day. *Majorian* gave me a great ride and it didn't matter that he was basically only there for the day out. His owner, Reg Morris, still is a great supporter of ladies' races. My career total for the year stood at only six but, with a very feeble third and fourth, I was second season leading lady rider. Once again I attended the presentation dinner at Woburn Abbey where I received a silver rose bowl presented by Lady Tavistock, Marchioness of Woburn.

We had a great start to '84 with two favourites of mine, *Pagan Sun* and *Wing and a Prayer*, winning at the Lincoln Meeting at Doncaster. *Pagan Sun* was a very nervous horse and, if he had been a human, would probably have been on valium. A long rein was always needed as he would rush in and out of his stable with such force, and it was a job to keep hold of him. Later on in the year I struck up a fantastic relationship with him that would see me miss my breakfast for the following two years. He was always bouncing about, even after exercise, and would not walk home sensibly. On arrival back at the yard all the others would be cool, calm and collected and be put straight back into their stables, but he would be hot and sweaty. I would have to wash him down thoroughly and walk him round until he was dry. By that time breakfast was over.

It seemed an age since the Dickinson days but my day at Aintree, this time as spectator and supporter for TC as he rode the good but awkward *Ambremont* over the National fences on the eve of the big day, brought it all close again. The sight of the runners approaching and then "flying over" the Chair made my heart skip a beat as I stood at the wing of the fence. The scope of these seasoned chasers and jockeys left me awestruck and my legs seemed rooted to the spot as I turned to watch the rest of the race on the big screen. *Ambremont* refused four or five fences out. He had had enough. From such fantasy of him winning, to finishing in the frame, to seeing a dejected but safe and not altogether unhappy TC is a lot to comprehend in such a small space of time. I learnt that the winning is undoubtedly the ultimate but "the thrill of the chase" is also something to savour.

Bootleggers Moll was always a little backward in coming forward, but the big black mare, who bore no resemblance to *Black Beauty* at all, gave me my first winner at Towcester in a national hunt flat race. She won by four lengths and it didn't matter that there was only one other opponent. She was a winner. We were very short staffed in the yard that May bank holiday, with runners and all the lads who had a licence managing to get a ride somewhere. It was no hassle for me. With help from the box driver Joe Todd, I changed into my colours, led *Bootleggers* up in the pre-parade ring, ran into the weighing room, weighed out, put the saddle on, put my helmet on, rode her, weighed in, washed her down and then got a friendly rollicking for returning home in my breeches. Not the done thing. Then, after about the twentieth time of giving Alan and Jan Bailey my step-by-step recollection of the race, eating some salad and speaking to TC (who had won the five twenty at Ludlow on *The Thunderer*), it was home, as my next day was to be an early start. I'd had a day to remember... a day to savour...

I opened my eyes, at 3am to be precise, to take *Wing and a Prayer* to Chester. This usual overnight trip had to be done in a day on this occasion. *Wing*'s eyes blinked in disbelief as I opened his door but this big strapping son of "*Oats*" (who had been a good racehorse) was so laid back that when any of the lads rode him a gallop, Alan used to say, he winked at him as he went past. Despite the early start, in the afternoon his black coat shone with such well being that the hundred pounds best turned-out was soon tucked safely in my pocket. Later in the year I rode him in a ladies' race at Lingfield, finishing fourth, and I was annoyed at myself for not being more forceful on him. I should have laid him up in a handier position so I was on the heels of the leaders as we began to descend the hill and swing into the straight. He was the best horse I had ridden so far, opportunities were few and far between and although I pushed and kicked him all the way to the line, valuable ground had been lost – as Alan told me on my return home.

At the end of the month I had my first ride over hurdles. It was at Fakenham on amateur day. I rode *Call Up*, a safe but relative novice who would never be in my list of favourites. This was not just because he unseated me at the second flight but also because he had been the instigator of a row between Alan and myself. *Call Up* had ability to win. He galloped with flat winners and we laid him out for a very lowly contest at Market Rasen. TC rode, the money was on and I stood in the stands with Alan to watch the race. At the third last *Call Up* began to drift out to his left after holding a handy position on the inside of the right-handed track. Coming wide round the bend into the home straight meant he had given away a lot of ground. There didn't appear to be anything wrong with the horse but TC reported he had hung so badly it had been hard for him to ride when they had really started to race. Alan was furious and blamed TC. It was an horrendous drive back to Newmarket, no one saying a word. Alan drove like a maniac, trying to work out how he was going to explain to the owner, who had put all the money on, how this "certainty" had got beaten. One of the down days in racing...

Three days later I overheard one of the lads saying that Alan had said TC hadn't even tried to win the race and that he wouldn't ride our jumpers any more. Now it was my turn to be furious. Alan had just stepped out of his back door as I was on my way to confront him. "How could you even think such a thing?" I squealed at him, and then rushed on with all the reasons why he wouldn't do that and especially not with one of ours and all he wanted to do was ride winners. Alan stood dumbfounded as emotion got the better of me and Jan appeared, wondering what on earth was going on. Anyway, the whole incident was sorted out and things returned to normal, the air well and truly cleared.

Call Up continued to work well. But one day up at the links with the other jumpers the lad answered Alan's question, "And what the 'eff were you doing on that?" with "I couldn't ride it, gov'nor, it was hanging so bad." Needless to say the horse never won a race even though he jumped well.

The yard had fallen on hard times but we struggled on. As long as I could tell Alan that all was well in the yard at the end of the day, then at least I'd helped in some way. He somehow kept as many of us in work as he could, and while he struggled with owners who all of a sudden found themselves unable to pay for half a dozen horses in training, and tried to find new owners, we seemed to be running round chasing our tails and not really getting anywhere. The good thing through those hard times was that we still managed to have winners. Also we'd been in dire straits before and it had passed.

My winner at Towcester seemed to have started the ball rolling, bringing my total of rides to five in May and, with an outside ride (for another trainer) I thought my career had started to move. However, I managed to get only three more rides by the end of September. I kept reminding myself I'd ridden a winner and next flat season I would have more confidence to ring up for rides. No gain without pain!

I learnt the meaning of a word in those times that I often look for now, loyalty. When the yard was flying and everything was running smoothly Alan would invite the staff in for drinks or even a party to celebrate a winner. We would often get finished early and if there was anything Alan or Jan Bailey could do for any of their staff then it was done! Now I found myself facing near mutiny. Some of the lads were moaning about wanting more money; these were lads who were getting rides, these were lads who, if they had been stopped wages when they had a day off or were late, would not have been able to pay their rent at the end of the week. One day three lads all walked out at the same time; we were better off without them. They were the proverbial rats leaving the sinking ship. But this ship was far from sinking, thanks to one of the owners who was starting to get into racing in a big way. Terry Ramsden stepped in, bought the horses we didn't want to lose and basically threw a life jacket round Wroughton House. It was the start of five glorious years.

Me at Bridlington 1962.

*Me, Anne and Elaine on Prince and Misty
after a day at the show 1969.*

Me and Prince 1969.

"Molojec" *Lucky at the last - my first winner over hurdles, Ascot, December 1986.*

Photograph by Action Prints.

"Planet Ash" *My first flat winner, Newmarket, July 1987. Led in by Wendy McLaughlin, Alan Bailey (trainer) on right.*

Photograph by Paddock Studios.

First running of the Queen Mothers Cup, May 1988. From left to right: Anthea Farrell, Sarah Easterby, HRH The Princess Royal, Myself, Sandy Brooks, Jenny Crossley, Julie Cecil (behind), Jo Winter, Franca Vittadini.

Photograph by Kenneth Bright.

Receiving 2nd season leading lady rider's award from the Marchioness of Tavistock, far right Reg Morris, October 1983.

Leading in "I'm a Driver" (who fuelled my dreams) after winning the Buchanan Gold Cup, Ascot, November 1978. (Jockey Tommy Carmody).

Photograph by Harold Stevenson (Provincial Press Agency).

Nine years later on "Jolliffe's Double" - he had given me my first ride on the flat at Doncaster and now my first ride over fences at Market Rasen, April 1987.

Photograph by Kenneth Bright.

"Great Gusto" *winning the Ladies Derby at Ripon, June 1989.*

Photograph by Fotosport (Racing).

Delighted in the winner's enclosure with "Great Gusto", owner Terry Jennings and trainer's wife Alison Thom.

Photograph by Fotosport (Racing).

"Fourth Tudor" *jumps the last in the TR colours and goes on to win by a head, Plumpton, August 1987.*

Photograph by Bob Williams.

"Beechwood Cottage" *winning at Redcar, May 1988.*

Photograph by Fotosport (Racing).

"Snickersnee" *winning at Yarmouth – first winner for Henry Cecil, July 1991.*

Photograph by P.H. Photography

"Howjal" My last winner over hurdles, Lingfield all weather, January 1991.

Photograph by Bob Williams

"Rose Glen" My last winner on the flat, Ayr, July 1991.

Photograph by Kenneth Bright.

CHAPTER EIGHT

The Glory Years...

The Bailey/Ramsden connection

Although it would still be a few more months before the integration of Ramsden's operation took effect, morale was high. The work load began to ease off as many things started to change, and all for the better as far as I was concerned. Pat Gibson came and took over as head lad. I would be able to concentrate more on riding, but first, two weeks on a Greek island called Santorini was in order. I left instructions for Pat to ride *Jamesmead*, who was now growing into a lovely character. His first run had been a promising one at Newbury under Pat Eddery. As things turned out *Jamesmead* moved to another trainer after a couple of runs. I often saw him at the races but horses soon seem to forget you and there is always another needing a place in your affections. By November I had my hands full looking after our new hurdling star. *Wing and a Prayer* won first time out at Kempton by thirty lengths. He frequently changed his legs and there seemed to be more improvement in him. TC was ecstatic. This could be the horse that would give him the recognition he deserved; although Alan, for once, was uncertain if *Wing* would be good enough for Cheltenham. This thought played a major role a few months later.

For now *Old Hubert* was on the lips and minds of most. He had been backed down from 33/1 to 5/1 favourite with sponsors Hills for the November Handicap and Alan could not see him getting beaten. But even with no hurdles in the way "certainties" are few and far between, and Hubert was another also ran.

Our move to Induna Stables in Fordham Road was imminent. I was very excited at the prospect of moving into the bigger yard. There would be more work but also more horses and that, hopefully, would mean more rides for me. I'd had a taste of winning and a pride-denting fall where I had been warned, "Let him see his hurdles and, love, don't sit up his neck." All the warnings of how different a race is to schooling at home made graphic sense to me as I slid along the Fakenham grass after only the second hurdle. The boys in the yard revelled in my incompetence and Alan hoped I'd never bother with hurdles again. My total of nine rides by the end of the year included two outside rides on the flat for different trainers. I rode at Ascot again, the occasion taking over from where I finished, nearer last than first.

Some of the lads and I went to Induna to make the stables ready so we could start moving the horses in. The plan was for them to move in after exercise but, with most boxes needing a good cleaning out, I went back and told Alan we'd be lucky to have them ready by the afternoon. The stables were bedded with paper which had become packed solid around the sides. All the bedding had to be cleaned out and the stables washed with disinfectant before any of the horses could be moved in. Operation clean-up began. It was not a job for the squeamish as a multitude of mice and spiders became homeless, the paper having made a warm nest for them in the winter. The four old stone stallion boxes at the top of the yard by the tack room were by far the best. I reserved two of these for *Wing and a Prayer* and *Pagan Sun*. *Pagan* was gradually getting better going in and out of the stable but caution was still needed.

The flat season had drawn to a close but, with a small string of jumpers and Alan buying yearlings like they were going out of fashion, the stables were busy. I enjoyed driving the yearlings and riding them away nearly as much as schooling over the jumps. Schooling a horse is educating it, from teaching it to walk, trot and gallop to jumping hurdles and fences. TC and I worked well together when it came to schooling over the hurdles. I always rode a lead horse and he the newcomer. It was satisfying when we schooled a young horse and it jumped well. The best lead horse of all time was *Jolliffe's Double*. He would go at any pace – fast, slow or in between. He would out-jump his young counterpart and a stride or so after the hurdle steady up and wait until they were back upsides. *Pagan Sun* was very keen in his work and, although it appeared we were stuck together with sticky back plastic, I was "jocked off" when it came to his first schooling session. But I still rode him over to the schooling ground which seemed to baffle Alan and TC. I was only too pleased that TC was schooling him, as that would just about secure the ride for him when *Pagan* made his debut over hurdles. He was a silly ass at times and, with being used to galloping round the links, he could get quite wound up. I have no patience with children or some adults but I was different with my horses, especially ones who were on the nervous side. *Pagan* needed lots of reassuring and however much he bounced around, pulled at the reins or sweated up, to sit quiet was the only way to ride him. I only rode him once in a race, finishing fourth.

He jumped well over the hurdles, a little too well, not touching a twig. I knew what he thought, clearing them half in fright in case one jumped up at him! We found out that the best way of settling him so he didn't pull too hard was to ride him right on the heels of the one in front, thus saving energy and hopefully helping him to stay the distance of two miles over hurdles, this being the minimum trip. I'd always dropped him well off the other horses when cantering or galloping but I had to be careful not to lay him too far out of his ground. He was working with *Wing and a Prayer* who by now had won and been second. My temper had flared on the latter occasion. I gave some man whom I'd never seen before a right mouthful (unlike me in public) as I led my horse towards the winners' enclosure, for accusing TC of dropping his hands. *Beat the Retreat* had won by a head up the Sandown hill and momentarily, when it seemed Steve Smith Eccles had the race in the bag, his mount began to tire quickly, TC had renewed his challenge which only just failed. The man turned out to be a T.P. Ramsden worker but through my naivety I never thought about any repercussions. Not that there were any, but I should have thought about TC's position before opening my mouth. Typical woman...

Pagan was a different type of horse to *Wing*. He was light and flighty, athletic. *Wing* was laid back and sturdy but by no means slow, his power just took time to reach its peak, while *Pagan*'s was instant. Trial gallops often happen and we were no exception. After sitting *Pagan* right on the heels of the big, nearly black horse, I cruised easily over the undulating ground. Setting off with the schooling fences on our right I wondered if I was riding the right horse as he relaxed in my hands only inches from clipping the hooves of the leader. I had to take a slight pull where the ground goes gradually downhill, left handed and alongside the railway. Then, relying on my lead to keep an even pace so I did not have to tug unnecessarily on his mouth, I hoped we'd missed the 8.00am Cambridge to Bury train! Pulling him out for daylight as we turned up the finishing straight, he flew past *Wing and a Prayer*, his speed settling the issue in a matter of strides. The big question was, would he perform the same way over eight flights of hurdles?

One morning soon after, Alan told us one of John Jenkins' owners was interested in buying *Wing*. He had aspirations of winning the Triumph Hurdle at Cheltenham in March. Alan for some reason did not think he would and Mr Ramsden said if they came up with the right money *Wing* would be sold. Despite our pleading, he was sold in January on the eve of the Triumph Hurdle Trial and a horsebox arrived to take him to Cheltenham. *Pagan Sun* was to make his debut in the same race and the two stablemates were now rivals. It was asking a lot of *Pagan* but if he was as good as we thought, he had to prove himself. I didn't want to lose either of them, they were a different type of horse and *Pagan* still had to stay the trip.

Money piled on *Pagan* and the punters latched on to the fact that the flamboyant owner who had sold his winning hurdler had a better one to play with. I stood on the stable lads' stand after leading my horse out onto the track and Derrick Morris, who was the travelling head lad for Jenkins, turned to me in disbelief as the odds shortened on *Pagan*. TC held *Pagan* up at the rear of the field settling him well although still quite keen, while *Wing* with his new jockey Steve Smith Eccles was handy and, as they raced round the big picturesque track, I willed *Pagan* to win. *Wing* took up the running and, as they began to approach the third last, the commentator said that the newcomer *Pagan Sun* had made ground to track the leader and was cantering (going very easy). TC shouted at Steve to go on a stride but his cheekiness backfired as *Pagan* blundered badly at the hurdle. From travelling strongly he went to jelly and, watching, we could all see his chance was gone. *Wing*, meanwhile stoked up, powered to victory. Alan gave the winner a pat on the backside as he came in off the track, which I thought was sporting, and I wondered if *Wing* had felt totally confused about all these strange people patting and hugging him. Did he wonder why I wasn't with him?

It would be a lie if we said anything else, we were totally dejected. Even if *Pagan* hadn't made the blunder it seemed unlikely he would stay two miles. Our hopes were raised a little when he annihilated his opposition on his next outing. Although the tight Norfolk track of Fakenham is a far cry from the festival and Cheltenham, he did win by 15 lengths. As things turned out, both ran in the Triumph Hurdle at the Cheltenham Festival in March, neither of them managing a place. *Pagan* then ran in the Lincoln Handicap at the first meeting of the new flat season that opens at Doncaster and, although unplaced there, he won a couple of other races and was placed a number of times. He settled beautifully in his second season over obstacles but only won at Fakenham; he just didn't see the trip out anywhere else.

I schooled him once when there was no other lead horse and he was magic, he jumped round the links like a gazelle. He took off so far away from the hurdle I didn't think he would reach the other side. I led TC and another jockey, Scobie Coogan, the full trip round the links. If you go too fast or do something wrong when riding, the older lads ridicule you – especially if you are a girl or an apprentice. They say, "Oh look out, got the wind in your hair," or "'eard the roar of the crowd 'ave yeh?" Well, I had the wind in my hair alright and there was not much I could do about it, or wanted to, and Alan had told me not to pull at him in case he knocked his legs. "You went a bit quick, don't you think, love?" said TC, as quiet as ever but still letting you know you'd done something wrong. Then Alan in contrast, "I didn't mean that 'effing fast, and before you ask, the answer's no!" By now he was grinning at TC, asking him how his horse was. It was mid summer and I'd had two rides since the turn of the year, the last being my second ride over hurdles and my first clear round on *Call Up*. Now everything I sat on I wanted to ride in a race, any race. It wouldn't have mattered if the horse had only three legs; if the trainer wanted me to ride it, then I would have.

Unfortunately, I hadn't had enough rides for other trainers to use me when there was someone more experienced available and, at that time, Alan just didn't have the right type of horse to run in an amateur race. But they would come, he assured me. I focused on working hard and learning everything I possibly could about the horses; it would be time not wasted. I always had a thing about wasting time and now I often wonder where the time went!

I'd started to ride a two-year-old second lot called *Beechwood Cottage*. He was a bit light mouthed and had had problems with sore shins. He was quite a plain chestnut but had a lovely character and provided a lot of kids with their first taste of winning. He also gave me my main bulk of rides over the next few years. The summer was busy and now, with up to thirty horses in training, winning was the main objective. Then somewhere among all this activity of going racing, night and day, ringing up for rides and a bit of office work, I was asked by the woman in the estate agents/building society if I wanted to sell my house. People were crying out for my type of terrace house. It didn't take a lot of thinking about and the "For Sale" sign soon went up. My friend Tess, who worked for another estate agent, told me about the new houses on Drinkwater Close, where she lived. If I went in straight away, she was sure there were a few plots left. They were after people who had already sold but they would put me on the list. Not very encouraging, and my house was on the market with a rival agent!

Then one morning over breakfast I was telling Alan I'd had a few people to view my house but had not seen anything else that I liked, except the new Drinkwater Close houses. I was just about to ride a two-year-old filly exercise second lot, when Alan told me I was 50s and drifting (a longshot) for one of those houses. However, he had done a bit of business with Januarys, the estate agents, and could recommend me, so I was to go and have a chat immediately. I sold my house in the next few weeks and secured plot 36. Imagine my horror when Tess showed it to me; it was only two bricks high. I lodged with a couple of friends, Sue and Andrew, until finally moving in October. It was worth the wait and I also saw it being built. I remember going round there and asking all sorts of questions about the buildings. In fact one of the workmen thought I wanted a job but I was just interested. Christmas was wonderful in my new home. Everything was in order and it was satisfying for me.

March was soon upon us and I rode at Doncaster. My horse *Winning Star* ran well to finish tenth. I had become close to the horse since he arrived in the yard the previous year, partly because Alan had told me I had to ride him out every day. He was being laid out for a gamble and a veil of secrecy surrounded him. I was often boxed up and leaving the yard before the first worker arrived, darkness still hanging heavy in the sky. Then, after legging the jockey up on Southfields or the Links, Alan and I would find ourselves whispering. The darkness would lift a little to reveal a thick fog. There was never a soul around to see or hear anything and, after realising this, we felt pretty silly. It was quite eerie as the sound of hooves and breathing came closer but, hard as I tried, the fog shielded the sight of horse and rider until they appeared nearly standing on my toes. The early morning excursions paid off when the gamble was landed at Market Rasen one very wet and cold

November day. I went into the house that evening to say that all was well with our winner and Alan asked me to see if there was a shirt in a small sized suitcase that was on the table. I lifted the lid, not really paying attention to what I was doing, and let out a loud gasp, shutting the lid quickly. I'd never seen so much money and, even on closer inspection, it didn't look real. I was assured it was. It was like being in one of those old black and white films: "Take the money and run, sweetheart, but you won't get very far before the boys gun you down!" After that, for a while anyway, every time we had a winner we'd say, "The money is in the suitcase."

Turning fortunes

Forty-eight horses were housed at Induna and, by May, seven winners had been turned out and a number of places. Terry Ramsden owned most of the horses even though we only had his second string, Mick Ryan training the great *Katies*. Our horses were proving that Alan Bailey was a trainer not to be taken lightly and then word came via the manager that six horses were leaving to be trained in America, where Terry owned a yard and stud. The worst thing about this decision was that all our winners were going, including *Pagan Sun*! Alan managed to save one, *Below Zero*. The morning they left I appeared at *Pagan*'s door around 3.15am to give him his feed and prepare him for his long journey. I scolded myself for getting upset and vowed never to get as attached to another horse again. Reports were not good about *Pagan* during his six weeks in quarantine and later on I heard he was turned out in a field somewhere over there.

My enthusiasm for race riding did not wane even though, when ringing up for rides, I was repeatedly turned down. I only managed to get two outside rides but it was two more than the previous year and, by the end of July, I'd had five and never troubled the judge. Unfortunately TC and trainer David Wintle had. An inquiry into the seemingly improved running of *Tierri Di Siena*, which won a lowly selling hurdle at Taunton, had been referred to Portman Square. Anybody who is accused of infringing the rules of racing has to appear before the Disciplinary Committee at the Jockey Club. They were both banned for the first three months of the jump season. They had been hard done by and the form book proved it.

We had a few nice horses to go jumping and after their first run at Warwick, *Justthewayyouare* and *Turn'em Back Jack* were entered at Market Rasen. Alan asked the owners and they said I could ride *Jack*. The other horse was well fancied and ridden by Declan Murphy. This was my third ride over hurdles and I was only just beaten for third place. I led till approaching the second last and was looking forward to my next ride before dismounting. I did not have to wait too long.

Later that month I was fourth on *General Concord* at Huntingdon, in the Ramsden colours. Although connections were delighted with our performance, this being his first run of the season, I knew that I probably would not be on board next time. Graham McCourt had become Ramsden's jockey. This meant he would ride all Ramsden's horses, from whichever stable they were trained unless, of course, as in this instance, he was riding one at a different meeting.

TC was still riding Terry Ramsden's horses and had ridden *Santropardre* in the Triumph Hurdle at Cheltenham. But Graham rode the best and later on, when we had some really nice horses of Ramsden's, I obviously wanted TC to ride. Sometimes it was very difficult for Alan. There was pressure on him to use various top jockeys when TC had already schooled them. The pressure was often from people who were working for Ramsden; we had been instructed to speak to them, not Ramsden himself. Yet he had already commended TC on being a good and loyal jockey, remembering, no doubt, the early days of *Ramo's Lady*. So why now would he not want TC to ride? Why would he give him the job of riding out his horses up and down the country, while being on his enforced holiday? It seemed to me someone didn't want TC to ride.

It upset me enormously... my involvement in work and private life unfortunately overlapped in this case, and kept me from voicing my opinion too much. Rides of any real quality were hard to come by and TC, forever the professional, knew that some rides were better than none. So we battled on as if on a mission, hoping, waiting for that "real good horse" to come along. So we can ride winners and be a winner!

Two new inmates had arrived. *Dunston*, a big, strong, flamboyant three-year-old colt and *Fourth Tudor*, who at four and gelded had the game pretty well weighed-up and was content with an easy life, not bargaining for a change of stables. I took to *Dunston* straight away. He had plenty of character and was quite bolshy, an attribute I like jumpers to have. The jumping game is only for the brave and bold! But it was *Fourth Tudor*, the fairly wishy washy chestnut, who would provide me with some very special times. Alan used to shout at me to keep *Dunston*'s head up as some mornings he would start to bronc playfully (like a bucking bronco) when something set him off as we were making our way over to Southfields. He never put any power into them and only ever did a few, showing his well being. When you ride a horse often you get to know all their idiosyncracies. I was never worried but Alan feared the strong robust colt would fire me into orbit. Both horses were schooled over hurdles and jumped well. Graham was delighted with them and rode *Dunston* at Uttoxeter first time out. He was a stayer on the flat and travelled easily, but he failed to quicken and finished second.

I was always pleased when we had a winner no matter who rode them, although I obviously preferred TC to have the chance. I was left in charge of the yard and the general running of things when Alan went on holiday. Alan and I both went through the entries and he nominated the races that the horses could run in, bearing in mind the winter sport can often be abandoned due to frozen ground. I would then liaise with Mick Miller who was now racing manager and go from there. *Dunston* had been disappointing. He all but fell at Chepstow and his last run at Cheltenham under Graham Bradley was less than inspiring. But I felt he was improving and hoped he'd come good. He was due to run at Huntingdon while Alan was on holiday but he was also in a novice handicap at Sandown later in the week, where he looked set to carry the minimum weight of 10st. I knew Graham couldn't do 10st and I knew from riding arrangements that he was probably going to a different meeting.

We arrived at Huntingdon and, after some overnight frost and no winter sun, the Clerk of the Course said there would be no fine if trainers wanted to withdraw their horses. I'd walked a good part of the course and suggested to Mick that we pull him out; he agreed. I spoke to Alan and he said to run *Dunston* at Sandown and that TC would ride. My subterfuge nearly paid off when *Dunston* ran a tremendous race, failing only by a neck to take the spoils. The Sandown hill again played a major role, making the difference between win and lose...

I was allowed to pencil in entries – which meant that not one amateur race, flat or jumping, went unnoticed – but I felt I was losing touch with the horses. I was now riding just one lot and spent the rest of the time in the office. It was good experience and I did the wages on the computer, spoke to owners and dealt with Weatherbys, the organisation that deals with all racing administration. But I would often find myself looking out of the window, watching second lot bounce out of the yard and wishing I was with them. Times were flourishing, we had plenty of staff and I had wanted to do the office racing side. So there I remained, seizing every opportunity I could to ride out, constantly being teased by some of the lads about how easy I'd got things "Sat in the office all day," as they put it. They seemed to forget I was always there before them and, more often than not, still there when they were on their second pint down the pub.

Sometimes I would have a disagreement with the computer and would have to send out SMJ (Save My Job) calls to Mark Madgwick, who promises faithfully to come and teach you everything when installing the wretched thing. Then, after a few weeks of getting by, a problem would arise just before I was going to switch it off and go home. Usually it would be something really major to do with entries or wages – the sort of problem that you have to fix even if it takes all night. So as the heart pumps faster and faster, a clammy hand reaches for the phone to make a SMJ call. I'd wager 90 per cent of Newmarket secretaries have made at least one of these calls and the other 10 per cent don't have one of Mark's computers. Then the first half dozen times you ring, you cry: "It's bloody engaged!" Or that infuriating woman says, as if she is sitting right next to the person you want to speak to, "The cellnet number you have called is not responding, please try again…"

Panic sets in, then he answers. I'm half rollicking him and half grovelling, and he is so laid back, "No worries, I'll be there in five minutes." I know it is more likely to be half an hour but he is on his way. Now I feel guilty for rollicking him because he is coming to SMJ. He sorts the problem out but you still don't know what went wrong. He says it was nothing and will definitely go through things with you next week but hasn't got his diary. Then he wants to know all the gossip about who is doing what with who and where and why... Next week never comes – you don't ever hold your breath waiting for Mark Madgwick!

The property market was booming in 1986 and, after seeing a run-down bungalow called Becklyn for sale at Kennett (one of the surrounding villages) that stood on about four acres but needed a lot of time spending on it, we knew it had to be a step forward. My house at Drinkwater went in the *Newmarket Journal* on Thursday morning and was sold by the afternoon. I was quite sad to leave but, for the first time since the days of Coley Road, Becklyn felt the right place to live. The plan was to build some stables and have horses at livery. Although neither TC nor myself had any intentions of giving up race riding at that time, when the right moment came, it would be a place we could possibly train from. There would be a lot of hard work to do before the land stopped resembling a jungle. My lodger Angie moved in with me as TC still lived in Wantage. It would take some sorting out but there was no time limit. It was our home and we had all the time in the world to put things right. I was happy to stay round Newmarket even though we looked at properties further afield. It was a pity there were no stables to begin with, as Alan had plenty of overflow, but I told him we would not have any stables until the following year.

My third place on the Polish-bred *Molojec* was a shade unfortunate in gambling terms. He had been pencilled in for a selling hurdle at Catterick but, after running so well in the flat race, there would be no point in going there as the odds would be too short. Instead he was re-routed for a novice hurdle at Windsor. I was pleased that Graham couldn't ride him and TC had a chance of riding a winner. We knew he had improved a lot from the flat race and backed him with confidence. His short-head defeat by *Camden Belle* could so easily have gone in our favour, but it didn't. And TC's comeback ride from his "holiday" could so easily have been a winner, but it wasn't. That's racing.

Molojec continued to improve and ran a brave race next time out at

Newbury. This time the winning margin of a short-head went in his favour. He was a lovely horse who was always willing to please and on December 13th 1986 he put a smile on my face that remained there at least a week. Winning my first hurdle race at Ascot in a 23 runner amateur handicap is something no one can take away from me. Always up with the pace, he jumped impeccably, apart from making an absolute horlicks of the last, and up the run in I prayed for nothing to pass us. I'd had the odd puff of happy baccy in younger days but nothing compared with this light feeling of euphoria. When I pulled up I pinched myself. Have I really won? Did I really do it?

Alan and Jan were in the winners' enclosure with Bob Cox, whose wife's name and colours *Molojec* ran in. He had told us off quietly for looking at some gold chains in the paddock before the race but was now beaming like a Cheshire cat. I wasn't a fan of his and I knew he didn't like TC but I reciprocated his smiles and pleasantries because that's how the game works to a certain extent. The congratulatory slaps on the back from the other jockeys and valets felt good and I knew TC would be proud of me. I used Brendan Powell's body protector and returned it, thanking him. TC joked later saying to him "Body protector rode a nice winner then!"

Full realisation came on seeing the photographs and how close to a fall I'd been at the last. Alan spread the photos out over the desk so we could choose the right ones and, when the phone rang for him, he told Jan he was busy. He wasn't but was letting me savour my win a little longer. I had really won and I did really do it, but it wasn't enough to keep the ride at Wetherby on Boxing day. It was a professional race so 7lb claimer Patrick Farrell rode because I could not claim. Unfortunately my behind the scenes sulks were vindicated when *Molojec* was unplaced. "You are on a hiding to nothing if you keep insisting to ride him," TC had said. "If he wins, it's expected, and if you are beaten, then you'll wish you had not ridden him." I emerged reputation intact with the lads, and with Alan saying I would have won if I'd been on board. One of those situations that you will never know and never be able to prove.

I ended the year with eight flat rides, two of them for other trainers, and three hurdles comprising two fourth places and my one winner. Unfortunately, my winner fired up enthusiasm only in myself, and not other trainers, and I didn't ride on the racecourse again until April the following year – but not for the lack of trying.

The year had reaped many rewards and the gamble on *Cry for the Clown* was no exception. This home bred two-year-old did not look to have too much going for him as he was a very nervous yearling with a parrot mouth. But the proverbial swan he proved to be, winning all three of his two-year-old races. I rode him a lot as a yearling and he turned out to be one of the best rides in the stable, as that sort often do. One particular work day stands out from the time before he made his debut. We were galloping on racecourse side, one of the best gallops in the country. It runs parallel to what's called the Rowley Mile, the stiffest straight mile in the country, where some of the trial races for two-year-olds are run, whose trainers think they could be classic material at three years. The first three-year-old classic races for colts and fillies are run only yards away from where we gallop the horses. I loved riding galloping there – you had to be able to judge the pace right and it is different from two-year-old to three-year-old, flat horse to jump horse. I always liked to discuss the gallop with whoever I'd ridden with to ascertain whether they thought we had gone the right speed. This particular time I was riding *Beechwood Cottage* who now, at three years old, was an ideal lead horse for the two-year-olds. Peter Bloomfield rode *Cry for the Clown* and work rider Ian (Smithy) Smith rode another two-year-old called *Lack a Style*. My instructions from Alan in this gallop were to jump off and let *Beechy* run. If the two youngsters could keep pace with me then that would be great, and if they could not then there would be nothing to get excited about.

I covered three furlongs and, although I could hear my pursuers, they had not become visible. Then as we swept into the dip before the final pull towards the winning post, *Beechy* began to quicken without being asked and in a matter of strides the two-year-olds appeared, first *Lack a Style* being ridden along quite vigorously and then *Cry for the Clown*, Peter sitting motionless with a double handful (going easy). I asked *Beechy* to quicken again, and he did but was now under pressure. If Peter had given his horse the office he would have gone clear without a doubt. The other horse hung onto *Beechy* but Peter was a good length up at the finish.

We thought *Lack a Style* would run well at Newmarket on the Saturday but were quite surprised when he won at 25/1. That could mean only one thing: *Cry for the Clown* was a banker in the seller at Ripon later in the week. He won easily and, like everything after the event, we all wished we had had a few more pounds on. I always liked setting up the two-year-olds when you knew they had ability and then running them in a class below. It was not often they would get turned over!

There was always a buzz when we had a winner and when a gamble came off it was even better...

The best of both worlds

I think Alan thought I might be offended when he suggested having another secretary in the office. I didn't do the book keeping and didn't want to; then there was the VAT to do and all those sorts of tedious jobs. I wanted to be racing, riding or studying form – not typing correspondence to some accountant, which I wasn't doing very well. "How about me becoming your assistant then?" I beamed at him, he couldn't say no. It was the perfect solution, so in February 1987 I became his assistant trainer. I was more use about the yard and being available to go and saddle up at the races at a moment's notice. I was back riding out two or three lots as well – much more my forte than typewriting!

Annabel Briggs soon settled in to her new post and I settled into mine. For me it was the best of both worlds. I was out with the horses all morning and, when not racing, there were riding out lists to do, entries to look through and I also started to keep a diary of all the horses' setbacks and ailments. We had invested in a laser for treatment and that was added to my list of jobs. The laser was used for a number of different ailments, from sore shins and bad backs to cuts and grazes. It proved to be a good investment and a lot of horses benefited from it. For Annabel it was good too; she re-arranged the office to her own liking, quite surprised no one objected, and we all worked well together.

I always liked to ride in the first amateur race at Doncaster in March but since riding *Molojec*, a winner back in the December, I hadn't had another ride. When I had no luck in getting a mount at Doncaster, I wondered if I ever would. My dreams of riding *Molojec* at Liverpool in the amateur hurdle race after the Grand National were soon squashed when it was announced that he would go chasing. As we only had hurdlers, somebody decided he would be better trained with a lot of other chasers. By the time Grand National day came he had moved to Mrs Pitman's stable at Lambourn. But he still ran over hurdles and, ironically, won the amateur race under Robert Bellamy, to give him his first winner too. As always, disappointments were soon shrugged off and by Easter it was almost forgotten. This was due to two entries, Turn'em Back Jack on the Saturday and *Jolliffe's Double* on the Monday, both in amateur races and both to be ridden by me. *Jack* fairly hacked up (won easily) and I felt I'd ridden a good race. Those Easter Eggs didn't half taste good on Sunday!

Alan wasn't too keen on me riding *Jolliffe* as it would be my first time over fences and only his third. Also he had failed to complete, being pulled up on the first occasion and falling on the second. Contrary to this he jumped fences well and we had done plenty of schooling. My bleating was getting on Alan's nerves, too, and I told him it was only a matter of time before my fencing debut, so he might as well get it over with. You are told a hundred times how different schooling is to the actual race, but it was something I didn't quite comprehend until the tapes went up and I was approaching the first fence on this nearly uncontrollable monster who had disguised himself as our sweet old *Jolliffe*. I wondered if I should have run the last mile and a half to the track, saddle and bag under arm while Jan Bailey sat in the Bank

Holiday traffic. Sedately popping round the links to fairly hurling ourselves at the first fence, I hoped this horse knew what he was doing, as my attempts to steady him were being totally ignored. With power and excitement, he jumped the first and I held on, aware of the time that we spent in the air. The second was upon us so soon but the Open Ditch held no fears for my horse as he launched himself into orbit and my head into the clouds. I held onto the reins but there was no communication. Bursting into speed I didn't know he had, his hooves made touch down and I felt as if he was showing me what he could do. I hoped the resemblance to a kamikaze pilot would soon pass as I imagined a close up of my face, lips stretching sideways to find my ears that were tucked safely under hairnet and helmet.

He changed back into *Jolliffe* by the time we jumped the water in front of the stands and I was pleased I had survived his enormous leap at the one before. He didn't seem to notice the horse and jockey that fell at the fence before the open ditch second time round, or the loose horse that decided to stay as close as possible to us at all costs and, after losing our position in the middle of the race, he ran on strongly to finish fourth. His exuberance helping him to keep up over the first few fences was disguised as speed and I told Alan he needed at least two and a half miles and would be better over three and even better in just amateur races! I had crossed another bridge but knew I had to polish up my act...

It was hard for me to do a lot of schooling as *Jolliffe* was our only chaser, but both horse and rider were more composed when we made our second appearance at Fakenham, again finishing fourth. Another Bank Holiday but that was just a coincidence. Some jockeys are referred to as "Bank Holiday Jocks", i.e. they only ride on Bank Holidays due to there being so many meetings on. I wouldn't be typecast into this category as it was more for the professionals. I looked forward to this particular day as all the races were for amateurs and Alan had entered three. Unfortunately *Jack* was lame but I was very excited about having two rides! On Saturday night I'd just finished eating a very generous helping of steak and chips when the phone rang. "Can you ride one in the selling hurdle on Monday and can you do 9st 7lb?" Adrian Chamberlain inquired. Yes on both counts, and I had three rides!

I was shocked when I weighed myself on Sunday morning. I was heavy, weighing 9st 3lb. I was planning on going for a run after riding out in the morning and now it would definitely be in a sweat suit. As it was Bank Holiday the appearance of a valet would be scarce and I didn't want to have to try and borrow a lighter saddle off anyone because I was a couple of pounds heavy. I had my own saddle that weighed 7lb so I needed to shed about 5lb. After doing my usual three-and-a-half mile run round the back of Kennett where I lived, and taking a hot bath, 3lb had disappeared. Another run in the evening would put me just about right, the intake of half a grapefruit and a black coffee being my only feed of the day. On Monday morning I weighed 8st 10lb, I had lost 7lb but it was only fluid. When I opened the paper the weights had gone up and my horse was now carrying 10st 10lb! This was because the top weight in the handicap did not run, so the next one moved to the top weight and all the others moved up accordingly.

I could have a coffee and a piece of toast now with my friend and then lodger Joss Drake before setting off to have three rides at Fakenham. It proved a lucky day for my friends Joss and Gary Honeywell who walked the course with me on arrival and I managed to tip them five winners. Alan had given me my orders as he would be at Sandown with our new sprinting stable star, *Hallgate*. He had won the Palace House stakes at Newmarket first time out and we were hopeful he would win again. We were becoming a very versatile stable. *Hallgate* was running in the Group 2 Temple Stakes, and we had a couple of other flat runners and the two jumpers. Their performances were equally as important to us.

Take the rough with the smooth

I held a slight advantage at the second last when my horse *Tiarum* blundered badly. Tanya Davis (now Sherwood) took the lead and I thought I would have to settle for second. I rolled up on the warm turf, not surviving a second blunder at the last, and I threw my whip down in disgust as I began to rise to my feet. Two more rides left to restore my pride and any faith the punters had in me! *Jolliffe* ran a great race to finish fourth behind Classified in the chase and *Justthewayyouare* was third in the last race of the day. I'd had a good day albeit winnerless. I ended the jump season with eight rides, two wins, one third, four fourth places and had hit the deck once. Riding over fences had been another achievement and my ambition now was to ride at Cheltenham. It is probably every jockey's dream to ride a winner at Cheltenham and Aintree.

The rides in amateur flat races were becoming more frequent with trainers ringing up for my services. The next month I rode for three different trainers at Warwick, Chepstow and Lingfield. *Reindeer Walk* for my old boss G.Huffer and *Gywnras* for David Wintle were to be the first of many. I travelled next to Edinburgh to partner *Not So Silly* but my first flat winner still eluded me.

The Newmarket July Friday evening/Saturday afternoon meetings soon arrived as did a wedding invitation from Chris Broad. Chris was TC's best friend so "Tone" was to be best man. I told TC that Alan had mentioned he might run *Planet Ash* in the amateur race but nothing was certain. If the horse ran I would miss the wedding. We worked too hard to give away even the slightest chance of riding a winner. TC wouldn't have done and he didn't expect me to.

The elation I felt on riding my first flat winner was incredible, especially at Newmarket and in the blue and white colours of T.P. Ramsden. I found myself thanking everyone who merely smiled at me. Brough Scott interviewed me live on television and the hard work, the slog, faded away as I basked in my euphoria. Alan's voice repeatedly said, "I said he'd win if you rode him like I told you." Peter Bloomfield went on to win the feature race of the afternoon on another Ramsden runner, *Cry for the Clown*, and a stable treble was completed at Nottingham that evening when *Tear It Down* won the seller...

I rode *Below Zero* in the Diamond race at Ascot finishing a distant sixth to the Princess Royal on *Ten No Trumps*. The traffic jam entering the racecourse made me very late and the rest of the girls riding were changed and ready when I arrived. I found the first available space to change into my colours and, in my haste, pushed aside a bag to make more room for myself. Then the owner of the bag appeared. "I'm sorry, I'm late," I said, trying to offer an excuse for invading her space. But the Princess told me not to worry about it!

Three second places in August put me with the top five leading lady jockeys in the country – all places being achieved on Alan Bailey trained horses. Three second places on three different horses at three different tracks with three different outcomes. *Planet Ash* finished second to a very good horse but Alan was not happy with my ride that day. I redeemed myself and also struck up a bit of a rapport with *Fourth Tudor* who was very laid back these days. One of the jockeys, Roy Carter, told me I'd have my work cut out and he hoped I was fit. I was fit, I assured him. I made sure of that and could often be seen running like a loony all over the place! As I made my way to the paddock, looking down to make last minute adjustments to my cuffs, a man's voice asked me for my autograph, handing me his racecard and a pen. I began to sign my name smiling to myself; this had never happened before! I looked up and was astonished to see the autograph hunter was Mark, my brother! I had no idea he was there. Each-Way backers, including Mark, were pleased with the odds of 25/1 and this type of race suited my horse who finished second.

Time had come round again to start schooling any three-year-olds we had to go jumping. As usual I rode the lead horse which this time was *Fourth Tudor*. He had a tendency to jump right, running a few strides down the hurdle before take-off. He'd done this when winning on both occasions as a novice. He made no attempt to jump straight even when I slapped him down the shoulder with my whip and I ended up getting a right bollocking from Alan. I think TC and Graham McCourt would have said something but they didn't need to after Alan told me to take the 'effing thing away if I couldn't ride it. I followed the next couple of times and he was a lot better. All in a day's work! On our next schooling session Graham rode *Fourth Tudor* and I rode one of the novices. "How come I'm riding this?" he inquired, "Does he run soon?"

"Yes," I replied, hoping he didn't ask me where.

"Go on, tell him where," TC's voice said. I threw him a look which said be quiet please! I didn't want Graham to know he was running in a ladies' race at Plumpton the following week. Alan wanted Graham to sort Tudor out and make him jump straight. He would not be too pleased schooling the horse and me having the ride in a race, as this does not go down too well amongst professional jockeys!

We had a variety of runners on August Bank Holiday Monday. *Fourth Tudor* was the only jumper and was favourite in the morning paper. He was the final leg of a treble bet, the other two being *Planet Ash* at Epsom and *Up The Kop* at Chepstow. Terry Ramsden had sponsored a series of ladies' hurdle races, this being the first one. It was marvellous for the lady jockeys and gave us a chance to show our jockeyship and ride a better class of horse. On saddling, Jan Bailey told me that the other two had duly won but I didn't worry too much. If Tudor won, he won, and if he got beaten, I'd get murdered at work in the morning! At halfway the partnership looked cooked as I scrubbed along in third place. But a brilliant jump at the last brought me within a neck of the leader and *Fourth Tudor* put his head in front on the line. It was the hardest ride I'd had up to now! And one of the most rewarding. A feeling of satisfaction and professionalism for doing my job well was now taking over from the excited light feelings that I had experienced with my previous winners.

Induna Stable's flag was flying high! We were turning out winners left, right and centre. Another milestone for Alan would be to train a winner over fences and, as we prepared *Not So Silly* for the Ayr Gold Cup (one of the most competitive flat sprinting handicaps of the year), I was nursing *Jolliffe's Double* to full fitness in anticipation of his first run of the season at Huntingdon. Jan Bailey and I nearly lost our voices while shouting home *Not So Silly* as he led close home to win the 1987 Ayr Gold Cup by a neck. And then we found ourselves cheering through tears of uncontrollable emotion as *Jolliffe's Double* jumped the last with TC riding and went on to win by eight lengths. Sheer unadulterated magic!!

We organised a party for the following weekend and celebrated long into the night. Alan always liked to have a party when we had a significant winner. This man who could be so ferocious and unreasonable was really very gentle at heart. *Jolliffe's* win gave him great pleasure and proved him right on two counts: for those who said Joe would never win over fences, now he had, and for those who said you can't train one chaser on his own, now he had.

Nothing could go wrong it seemed and after riding *Fourth Tudor* in a flat race, finishing fourth, I saddled yet another winner for Alan. Then, while looking through the entries I saw the race of my dreams. It was the perfect race for *Jolliffe*. A three-mile handicap chase for amateur riders at Cheltenham. The plan had been to retire *Jolliffe* even though he was a relatively young eleven-year-old. But he had blossomed since his win so Alan said I could enter him. He knew how much it meant to me and he quipped that "Seeing as he had turned out leading apprentices he might as well try with a Fat Ammy." That was our nickname for amateurs, especially if any rang up for rides. Whoever took the call would shout to Alan "Fat Ammy on the phone." "No," was the reply. Even though I rode all the Induna stable horses that ran in such races, people would still ring up for them.

It was some feeling walking round the parade ring at Cheltenham. If I'd had a thousand wishes, not one would replace this moment. I think *Jolliffe* felt the atmosphere too as he jogged lightly, head tucked so far into his chest I could hardly see his ears that pricked intelligently; he could easily have bounced into a dressage ring looking the part. He took a strong hold going to post and I hoped he would be sensible, unlike the ride he had given me at Market Rasen. You cannot take liberties with the Cheltenham fences. I was to ride him handy even though there were only six runners, taking full advantage of the low weight I carried, which was 9st 7lb. We set off in the middle of the picturesque course to jump a row of three fences before swinging left-handed toward the stands, which, next time round, would see us finish up the famous Cheltenham hill. We never got that far. He stood off the first fence, jumping out of my hands much too soon and although settling in-between fences, as he approached the wings he attacked them aggressively. He landed after the second with a thud, which made my helmet squiff to one side and as I pushed it back into place, one of the lads looked across at me fearing the same as myself. We approached the fourth fence in third place and this time he jumped well, not exerting himself too much but he got low at the next. His back legs hit the fence and catapulted me over his head. Then, as he nearly lost his balance on landing, his hind legs did the splits. He galloped off after the others leaving me to watch, my Cheltenham dream over...

He was lame on one hind leg but the course vet thought he would be okay. After a couple of days of being permanently tied up and x-rayed it surfaced that *Jolliffe* had broken his hock. We could see he was in pain and our vet Rob said he would have to be put down. I hid in the house like a coward until the deed was done. In pursuit of my ambitions he had lost his life and that most certainly was not a good feeling. My only excuse or consolation (or was it just to make me feel better?) was that *Jolliffe* loved his racing. His zest in the end was his downfall.

My first outside ride over hurdles was at Ludlow in another ladies only race. There was a lot of larking about in the changing room before the race and a practical joke made us roar with laughter. We told Penny Ffytch-Heyes to check she could see out of her goggles – we'd stuck a bit of paper in them so she couldn't see after she told us her horse was a bit dodgy, i.e. no brakes, didn't jump well and steering was suspect. But the trainer had told her to ride a race on it and she should be alright! There were no mishaps and for me it was one of the most exhilarating of my rides. We raced so tightly down the back straight that you could not have squeezed a cigarette paper between us and, as we approached the middle hurdle, Lorna Vincent was there on my inner; "I'm here Murgy, keep straight!"

We bounced off the fast ground at speed, our experienced horses jumping with flair and precision. What a feeling... Finishing down the field belied what I had just experienced. *Nippy Chippy* had been foot perfect until a mistake at the second last put paid to any chance of being placed. The standard of riding was very high and, although girls were continually knocked by the men in and around racing, we battled on giving it our all. I felt proud and privileged to be riding against such girls as Lorna Vincent, Gee Armytage, Tanya Davis, Diane Clay, Nicky Ledger, Candy Morris, Penny Ffytch-Heyes and Jessica Charles-Jones, to name but a few. Of course, there was the occasional mistake but you cannot say this never happened to the men either!

Riding two at Folkestone for David Wintle was another step in the right direction. If I could get placed on *Christo* in the amateur race there would surely be a few more. I finished third after three miles and three furlongs in heavy ground on a lazy horse, proving my fitness. This also helped me ride one of the best winners to date. A fourteen runner ladies' race at Huntingdon over two-and-a-half miles. The last in a seven race series sponsored by T. Ramsden. Jessica Charles-Jones couldn't be beaten overall but I fancied my chances against her well backed, Mrs Reveley trained mare. After jumping two hurdles I had to start pushing Tudor along. Barney Curley and Neville Callaghan said to Alan they hoped he hadn't tried to get his Christmas money out of us as we had no chance! Passing the stands with a circuit to go, I stuck to the inner and, as we swung right handed on this flat galloping track, I was last of a quintet to draw a couple of lengths clear. I pushed, urged and slapped, not making any ground but neither was I losing any. I passed Gee and, as the leaders lay three abreast at the third last, I was right on their heels. Destined to be fourth, with riders like Sara Lawrence, Sharron James and Jessica in front of me, I had to work harder than ever. Only a length down and on the inside at the second last (who said ladies' races are not entertaining) we chased Sara and Jessica in between the last two flights. Tudor showed his alertness this time, justifiably going right, setting himself up to jump the last hurdle quick and clean, landing a head to the good.

He almost came on the bridle up the run-in, sticking his head out to beat *Isaac Newton* by a neck. If he could talk he would have said, "Relax! don't panic, everything is under control". Mark Madgwick in horse form!

It was my finest hour... Alan, so proud, and me so pleased I had not let him down with his two fellow trainers ready to ridicule him for backing a woman in a women's race, and *Fourth Tudor* so laid back about the whole affair he was near horizontal!

I finished the year with two rides for David Wintle at Newton Abbott on Boxing Day. Unfortunately TC was sidelined through injury. Racing is sometimes a fickle game – if another jockey happens to win on your horse, there is always the risk of losing the ride. I was more than happy to ride then and it started to work out with a few trainers that, where possible, if TC couldn't ride, then I would. I'd more than doubled my number of rides from the previous year and riding against professional men and women had improved my riding of a race. With a total of fifteen jump rides and twelve flat, including four winners, I was enjoying riding under both codes.

Leading for one hour in '88

The first six rides of the year were for different trainers and included a win over hurdles on *Topori* for David Wintle, then a win on the flat riding *Beechwood Cottage* in a six furlong sprint the very next day! My orders were to keep him covered up and held up, not making a move until the two furlong marker. With a good draw three off the rail we were hopeful, but Alan had pondered whether to run him as he seemed a little quiet and looked set to carry top weight of 11st 7lb. At half way we were clear, all cover had dropped away tamely and, although they called a photograph, *Beechy* had won by half a length. Riding a flat winner so early on in the season gave me hope of doing well in the Ladies' Championship, especially now as I was riding for a number of different trainers. Another win at Chepstow a couple of weeks later saw me take the lead in the Championship for one whole hour, thanks to *Beechy*! This time over seven furlongs he burst out of the stalls so keenly that I didn't have a chance to cover him up. I looked round with three furlongs to go as I went into the lead, fully two furlongs too soon – nothing could lay up and *Beechy* won by four lengths. He was an enigmatic little horse who could have got me into a lot of trouble racing in this enthusiastic way, as the riding instructions were always to hold him up and cover him up! But our two victories occurred even though I was unable to carry out my riding instructions to the letter... nonetheless victories they were! Wanting neither to disappoint my exuberant partner nor to ignore my trainer's orders my initiative as a horsewoman and jockey was to ride the race as I saw fit.

Jo Winter (daughter of Champion jumps trainer Fred and my closest rival) rode her second winner of the year later on that afternoon, and this put her back in front in the Championship. Before I left Chepstow I'd got another ride in what was the first running of the Queen Mother's Cup at York. Carolyn Eddery recommended me for it as she couldn't ride on that particular occasion. Even though I finished last it was magic – riding at a top track in what was to become the second most prestigious ladies' race of the year.

One of the highlights of the year came in August when I was picked as reserve for a Newmarket Pro/Am race. This race (the only one of its kind) was sponsored by that marvellous supporter of lady jockeys, Reg Morris. To ride against male professionals on the flat is unique for amateur ladies and, although we had a strong team, we had to accept defeat, with the nearest lady placed being the Princess Royal who finished fifth. We were no answer to the men's team who were Pat Eddery (Champion Jockey), Paul Eddery, Michael Roberts, Tony Ives, Bryn Crossley and winner, Michael Hills. Another experience for me to savour.

Riding at two different meetings in the same day was a first for me. This came with a ladies' race at Redcar, Cleveland (2.15pm) and an amateur event at Lingfield's evening meeting in Surrey. Thanks to Alan, who drove me between venues (we didn't speed, honest!), I arrived in time to sit down and have a cup of tea, hoping that the horse I was about to ride for Graham Thorner could run as well as the white BMW 5 series that had taken me there.

Life was busy but fruitful, in terms of satisfaction. I had ridden in almost every ladies' or amateur race that was run, Jo Winter and myself clocking up eighteen and nineteen rides apiece (nearly ten more than any other lady riding) and still with more to go. This included Carolyn Eddery, Amanda Harwood (now Perrett), Elaine Bronson and Jane Allison, who had all ridden two winners. It proved to be an exciting battle for the Championship, with the lead changing several times.

The Championship went right to the wire at Folkestone at the end of October. Carolyn Eddery went into the afternoon in the lead but could have been beaten by any one of four, Jo her nearest rival, Amanda, Elaine then myself. I had only the remotest chance as two winners were highly unlikely. My rides were moderate and very moderate to say the least. Not even I could dream of being champion that day! It was the first time I experienced any atmosphere in the changing room, when a male jockey gave his fancied ride to Jo. She had to win with Carolyn unplaced, but any ill feelings were changed to smugness as Jo finished second. I sympathised with her. If the same situation had come my way, I would have grasped it with both hands. You may only have that one chance of being champion. As my friend Jennie Crossley found when the previous year she had come so close to victory, only to have it snatched away in one breath-taking moment. The decider ended in a photo finish that took twenty minutes to announce. She had failed by a short-head to win, thus enabling Carolyn Eddery to be champion by one point even though Jennie had ridden three winners to her two. The Ladies' Championship for flat racing works on a points system. Points were awarded to the first four; 10 for a win, 5 for second, 3 for third, 1 for fourth. After that the points were changed so it would be impossible to have more points with less winners.

My confidence had built up more and more through the season and I frequently rang for rides if my own stable didn't have a runner. The race I'd won the previous year had plenty of entries and I studied it closely. "Mr Thom," (yes). "Hello, it's Sharron Murgatroyd. Are you fixed up for *Bingdon Builders* in the amateur race at Newmarket on Saturday?" I had decided this was the best line to use – then the trainer could answer yes or no and knew who and what you wanted straight away.

"She's very strong," came back the answer.

"So am I. Would you like me to come and have a ride on her before the race?" I'd never spoken to him before but I knew his wife Alison. He didn't need to see me but I got the ride and he became another trainer for myself and TC to ride for.

It was a very cold November day at Nottingham and the three-and-a-half mile hurdle race on heavy going riding very moderate horses saw eleven girls lining up. The prospect of being covered in cold muddy earth or even being buried in the soggy ground by half a ton of horse is not everybody's idea of fun. Our spirits were further dampened by the recent fall of a colleague, Jessica Charles-Jones, who had sustained an irreparable back injury. This was a constant reminder of the danger we faced whilst taking part in the sport we loved. Our thoughts were with Jessica one moment, the race was with us the next. Perhaps, in our ignorance, we thought it could never happen to us as we carried on in our quest for winners.

Although I had been in second place in the Championship for most of the season, I slipped down to fifth by the end of the year. I rode a number of placed horses, but my two early season wins were the only ones I had.

Riding on the crest of a wave

Plenty of hard work, heart and soul had been put in at Becklyn and the place was looking much smarter than when TC and I had bought it in 1986. Stables had been built to our own specification and Mick and John Carroll (TC's dad and brother) had stayed throughout the summer working outside until failing light stopped them. They taught me how to mix cement when I was on hand to help and I laid the odd brick here and there, proclaiming later "look at the stables I built!" much to their amusement (sometimes). Their unstinting help was much appreciated and, without it, the completion of

Becklyn's stables, lounge and utility room would have taken much longer – if it had been completed at all. We had a few horses in livery from Induna but they didn't interfere with my job at Alan's or the race riding. Nothing at the moment could; our dedication to racing was second to none. We shared the work and, for a time, Becklyn was a mini version of "The Waltons".

"Goodnight Mick;"

"Goodnight Sharron;"

"Goodnight TC;"

"Goodnight Pa;"

"Goodnight Joss," and then all in unison,

"Goodnight John boy!"

But that was only if I had not already gone to bed "with the face on", tired and needing my sleep, wanting to be fresh for all the challenges that came my way.

It may have been a freezing cold Saturday in March but I hadn't really noticed. I set off after breakfast, heading north for Doncaster races, smiling to myself about the conversation TC and I had had when riding plans were finalised. "How many rides have you on Saturday?" I asked him playfully.

"Just the one." He knew what was coming next.

"Do you want to know how many I have?" He played along, not spoiling my moment.

"How many rides do you have, love?"

"Just the four," I beamed. It was the first time and I was pretty ecstatic. Four rides for four different trainers. The first in a novice hurdle for the late Jack Morris, then one in the seller (the winner is auctioned after the race) for Bill Perrin, *Turn'em Back Jack* in the handicap hurdle for Alan Bailey (his first run since I'd won on him at Southwell), and one for Jim Harris in the National Hunt flat race. It was highly unlikely I would visit the winners' enclosure but, as they were all professional races, I had a lot to live up to.

Unfortunately, my day ended at the first hurdle in the first race! I came round, after being concussed, in the ambulance room and repeated several times that I was alright to ride *Jack*. Of course I wasn't and was signed off riding for seven days. When TC asked if I was alright, I told him yes, not asking for any sympathy, just looking a little pathetic. I laid out on the settee, knowing that the falls are all part of the job. "How many rides did you have on Saturday?" he asked cheekily...

A week later I was passed fit and rode *Jack* at Chepstow. TC's sister, Mary, and her boyfriend, Robin, were living with us at this time and I gave her a lift as far as Membury service station. She was visiting her sister for the weekend. It wasn't often I had company on my journeys from Newmarket to the more distant jumping tracks. I always seemed to have a ride when none of the other lads from Newmarket did. I pulled *Jack* up on atrociously heavy ground.

My next seven rides comprised three jumpers, all finishing third, and four on the flat – three were second and the other won. I made my first trip abroad to ride and loved every minute of this Viennese experience. I stayed at the Hotel Intercontinental, wallowing in the luxurious surroundings, a million miles away from the normal routine of mucking out horses before going to the races. Unfortunately, as it was a Bank Holiday, the Spanish Riding School with its splendid Lippizaners was closed to the public but I did get a glimpse of a couple of them as I walked past. My ride finished second and I was whisked back to the airport. That evening back in Newmarket it seemed like a dream.

Being booked to ride at Haydock, three weeks in advance by Malcolm Eckley, was particularly satisfying as the owner had bred the filly himself. *Burnditch Girl* would never catch the eye on looks but she stayed on gamely, showing tenacity in the heavy ground to win. She also gave me my first flat winner for an outside stable. The journey home didn't seem to take half as long!

Even though Vienna was wonderful, the highlight of my year was riding in the Ladies' International at York. I felt proud to represent the UK against the European girls and there was a real buzz in the changing room as we put on black caps and our rivals donned the gold. With Jennie Crossley as our captain the rest of the team were Amanda Perrett, Carolyn Eddery, Jo Winter and Elaine Bronson. Amanda rode a brilliant race on *Deputy Tim* to win and I chased her all the way, finishing second on *Miss Sarajane*. Elaine and Carolyn finished third and fourth. The UK team was victorious and our prize of six bottles of Lanson pink champagne and a silver photo frame depicting two horse heads, was very much appreciated. But the sheer pleasure of basking in glory was enough for me.

In one month I had ridden a flat winner, ridden in Vienna, ridden for my country and now I was riding *Topori* in a hurdle at Fakenham; hoping for a repeat performance of the year before. It was not to be, but finishing third was no disgrace. The jumping season came to a close with a ladies' hurdle at Stratford. This time I rang Mr Eckley asking for the ride on *Tarpromise*. He was a big powerful horse and looked magnificent but, because he was so strong, he wore a citation bridle which would help me control him better than an ordinary bridle. It was normal for us to exchange a bit of banter while changing and a couple of the girls breezed in asking, "who's riding that thing of Mr Eckley's?"

"I am," I said, knowing they were going to wind me up.

"No doubt you'll be making the running, the way it's dragging the lad round the paddock!" I mounted him on the track and he cantered to post like a Christian. The tapes went up and I held him back in about fifth place. He flew over the first and I was happy, in control, but he pecked at the second and it was my turn to fly, straight over his head. Speed and momentum rolled me over and over. I waited for a good kicking from flaying hooves, aware of the number of runners behind me, then for the thundering sound to pass; I emerged unscathed, my pride taking a bigger battering than my body. But for Stephanie Baxter, who fell later in the race, it was a broken collarbone and Di Clay, who was kicked by a horse after she had fallen, suffered a back injury that put her into retirement for a while.

Two weeks later I was back in the winners' enclosure with my most notable prize to date. I won the Ladies' Derby on 20/1 chance, *Great Gusto*, and Stratford was put down to experience, gone but not forgotten! *Great Gusto* was trained by David Thom and owned by Terry and Wendy Jennings, and they provided me with plenty of rides after that. *Great Gusto* was third later on in June and I ended up having twelve rides that month. I was picked to ride in the Pro/Am race but, as this race fell on the same day as an amateur race at Redcar, Di Jones and I opted to go to Redcar where our finishing places would earn us points for the Championship. We were between the devil and the deep blue sea because, although it was good to ride in these races you did not earn any points. It was unfortunate that the races were on the same day.

Our schooling sessions on the Links had become a regular occurrence again on Sunday mornings. This particular morning I was riding *Turn'em Back Jack* to lead TC on the novice Dollar Seeker and Sean Woods on one of Rae Guest's novices. The last three hurdles had been replaced with new style plastic ones and I suggested that we take our horses to look at them to avoid inadvertantly surprising them later. "They'll be alright," the others said together. I muttered something about them calling themselves professionals and then they said to each other, "Oh, we'd better go and look at them otherwise we will never hear the last of it!" I walked on in front of them but knew they were having a giggle at my expense. There were quite a few spectators and they gathered by the last three hurdles. I led over the first five hurdles and they joined me on the bend to face up to the last three. By now we were travelling at a good pace and, as we approached the first plastic hurdle, I felt my horse (who was very experienced) begin to look and hesitate slightly. I urged him on and the three horses seemed to take off together. But somehow in mid air Dollar Seeker changed his mind and went through the wing of the hurdle, smashing it to bits. Thankfully both horse and jockey were soon on their feet, albeit a bit dazed. One can never predict what will happen as horses have a mind of their own. Although we had taken every precaution there had still been a mishap and they thanked their lucky stars that I couldn't say "I told you so!".

I pleaded with Alan to let me ride a novice I had been schooling. Alan owned *Barnack* so he could make no excuses. TC was riding *Another Boy* for us in the same race and in the end Alan agreed, if Declan Murphy could not ride. In the meantime I had a call from Clive Brittain's office for me to ride in the last amateur flat race of the season. I took the chance to ride for this big stable, and I made the right decision. Alan told Mrs Tanner, a lovely lady and the owner of *Another Boy*, that her horse would jump round Aintree but he ducked at the first hurdle, unseating his rider. The lady nonchalantly asked if it was the low flying aeroplane overhead that had put her horse off! *Barnack* was the subject of a Stewards Inquiry after running so slowly and Declan told them he had been on faster donkeys! So I was glad that I was not there.

Whilst I was having the time of my life and looking forward to 1990, now daring to hope I could even be Champion, the recession was slowly creeping into everything. A lot of our smaller owners were finding things increasingly difficult. Terry Ramsden, who owned three-quarters of the horses in the yard, had been responsible for the rise of Induna and looked set to be the cause of its fall...

CHAPTER NINE

The Tears

We celebrated Christmas and welcomed in the New Year, in our usual way. The New Year's ball in Newmarket was a terrific party and we had a wonderful time. We were bitterly disappointed, though, when we arrived at Cheltenham on New Year's Day to find that *Ardesee*, TC's only ride, did not run because of the firm ground.

Pressure in the yard mounted even though we tried to push it away and one by one I watched people leave. Peter Bloomfield had already left, soon followed by Jimmy Quinn and Francis Norton, the three jockeys, who went to other jobs with Alan's blessing. It was sad to see the horses go. One minute there seemed to be a yard full, then by June only half a yard full. I'd only had seven jump rides but, on the last day of the season back at Stratford, I got the ride on *Tiber River* for Charlie Brooks. I was really pleased and even though TC was riding at Market Rasen's evening meeting, he came to Stratford hoping to see me ride a winner. It was not to be – I finished third. We drove on to Market Rasen for the 9.00pm and, as the light began to fade, the curtain closed on the 89/90 jump season. It seemed to take forever before we left the track and then we had to stop in a nearby village to satisfy the hunger pains that were now screaming at us. It was a regular occurrence that food was the last thought on a day such as this. Philip Barnard, who travelled back to Newmarket with us, weighed in with the fish and chips. He had now joined a jump yard after doing so well riding on the flat for the Piggotts, but before capturing any major prizes. This sport that can be so rewarding is also very cruel, and Philip lost his life after a fall on Boxing Day '91. It was going on for 2am by the time we finally settled down. It had been a long day but no one was complaining.

My ambition to ride more winners and be Champion was beginning to take me over, even though I never touted the fact except for my constant ringing up in search for rides. I felt a little frustrated at times and somewhere during that summer, when the workload and pressure from both Induna and Becklyn got to me, I wondered what I was doing wrong. No one around me seemed happy and I felt that there was only me to hold things together. This led to me making mistakes. I returned home in floods of tears one day after Mick McLaughlin, our travelling head lad, had given me a right rollicking because I had forgotten to declare a filly his wife Wendy was going to ride at Chester, her home town. He shouted that if I'd been riding it this would never have happened. It was not his outburst that made me so upset but my own inadequacy. She, too, was obviously upset; rides came few and far between for her and she was a grafter and a half, all 4ft 10in of her. TC told me not to worry but I felt awful, I couldn't do anything right!

My decision not to go on holiday with TC may or may not have been the first step to the breakdown of our relationship but without a winner and only two places by July, I didn't want to miss any races. I rode two for David Chapman and, even though they were unplaced, another connection had been made. I'd again ridden in the York International and with every year the competition for the Championship became greater. A couple of years previously two or three winners would have secured the Championship; now it was five or six. I tried so hard but could not force any one of my charges heads in front. *Ain'tlifelikethat* just about summed up the way things were going when I rode him at Ascot, finishing last. But that day anybody who had any feelings at all were with Lydia Pearce.

Ten thousand different lady jockeys (myself included) had rung up for the ride at Ascot on the John Gosden trained *If Memory Serves*! Lydia was chosen and, as we were unsaddling, I was really pleased my long time friend had captured such a big prize in winning the Diamonds. I was summoned to the Weighing Room for a Stewards' Inquiry and they asked me if Lydia had interfered with my horse in the first furlong. I had been aware of a horse crossing in front of me but in no way had it caused me to check. Melanie Morley was also in the inquiry and she too had not felt any interference. It was like being a naughty schoolgirl waiting for the Headmaster to return with our punishment as we waited for their announcement. We were called back in and were told that, although interference had not taken place, Lydia had broken the rules by crossing her field in the first furlong and they had no alternative but to disqualify her and place her last. The chance of riding a winner in this race may only come once in a lifetime and the lump in my throat rendered me speechless. I could offer no comfort, only a hand on her shoulder.

Autumn arrived and things at Induna stables were struggling on. Enough horses remained for four of us to ride three lots each and I was back as acting secretary but preferred to be out in the yard. I was still searching for that first win of the season but Saturday would be St Leger day and after that ladies' race there would not be many more. As we wandered down the side of the Harry Wragg sand canter, Maxine Juster (now Cowdrey) shouted across to me that Henry Cecil had been ringing for me to ride for him at Doncaster on Saturday. Just my luck, I thought – when I am not in the office the bloody phone rings for me. Then, moments later, Mr Cecil appeared, asking me if I had a ride on Saturday. I told him no and he booked me to ride *Exceptional Bid* who was owned by the (now late) Charles St George. It was a great feeling to even be considered to ride for the champion flat trainer. I drove to Doncaster with Lydia, Maxine and Jane Armytage. Lydia won on *If Memory Serves* (a just reward) and I finished fourth. It was a tremendous feeling seeing my name down to partner a Cecil-trained horse. Lydia and I celebrated with a bottle of champagne and cheered our good fortune. If we had said ten years before, that one day I would be riding for Cecil and she would be riding for Gosden, we would have been laughed at! We decided then that every winner was to be celebrated, as you never know when it would be the last.

The last few races of the season were pretty uneventful and riding only one more third place was disappointing. I rode *Exceptional Bid* at Haydock and he was my twenty-seventh ride of the flat season with no wins. Mr Cecil told me he would have a few to run in ladies' races the following year, so the dream of being champion was rekindled and my disappointment began to fade. Julie Cecil and Franca Vittadini, who had been on board up to then, would be hard acts to follow... But first a cold hard and lonely winter lay ahead, filled with pain and sadness. I wondered at times if I would ever be able to stop crying... stop feeling so alone... I had everything but felt I had nothing...

In October it became evident that TC and I would go our separate ways no matter how hard I tried for us to stay together. If they played "You've Lost That Loving Feeling" on the radio once it must have been on a million times. By the beginning of December I knew in my heart that there would be no reconciliation. TC must have prayed for the end of time like in the Meat Loaf song. After confessing everlasting love until the day we died, he was now praying for the end of time so he could end his time with me.

"Don't you hear me crying, oh babe, don't go... And don't you hear me screaming how was I to know." "For crying out loud you know I love you."

"Baby you can cry all night but it won't change the way I feel! And I can't lie... I can't pretend…"

I could not believe how my emotions took me over. One day so strong, almost blase about the whole situation; then so weak, shutting the door and wallowing in my grief... And he hurt too, I could see that.

My own personal upheaval led me to make other drastic changes and I left my job at Alan Bailey's after nearly ten years. He was now down to a handful of horses and really there was not enough work for me to earn my pay. I was still on hand to help if needed and regularly rode out for him. I felt I needed to be freer to do my own thing and now, instead of being tied to set hours in one job, I could ride out if I wanted to or just go straight to the races. I felt like I was deserting him; after all, he had given me the chances, he had advised me, he had trusted me, he had boosted my morale and given me confidence; in many ways he had been a father to me. Now the well was nearly dry and already I was looking for greener pastures. But he understood and I knew his and Jan's door was always open.

If race riding had been my vocation in earlier years, it was even more so then. Riding *Sphinx* in a ladies' race at Nottingham for Ray Bostock was the first of many outings for the King's Lynn trainer. Every ride in a professional race was a bonus for me and for the next few months I drove the forty minutes journey to his stables, where I would ride out four and sometimes five horses in the mornings. I felt I earned what race rides I had. It helped Ray, as his head lad Des was off with a broken leg, and it was good for me. But sometimes I wondered if it was all worth it on freezing cold mornings when we would be trotting down the bleak country roads, hands numb and feet ready to drop off for the fourth time that day, or when I'd had a particularly awkward ride round the gallops. I was being stretched to my limits both emotionally and physically and, although often disappointed at being replaced by professional jockeys, I still wanted to play the game. It was worth it, again and again, and when Ray said I could ride one in a race, I'd already forgotten that I'd been so cold inside and out.

The drive back home to do a couple of liveries of my own, or straight into Newmarket to ride out one in the afternoon for David Thom, then on to clip out the coats of Sean Woods' horses, was often hurried, as the light soon faded. In the winter months all horses have their coats shaved off, so they don't catch cold standing with wet long hair after exercise. I tried to fill every minute of my day doing something or going somewhere. Jennie or Joss never minded if I fell asleep in their armchair or sofa after missing the end of a video, then saying that it was good, but they did become increasingly worried as my weight slipped down to 7st 9lb, even though I was fit and strong physically. My riding had always been strong but now I was very aggressive, always having to try that little bit harder on the horses I was riding.

It seemed to be nearly dark as I looked out of the weighing room window at Sedgefield. I hoped the light would not fade too soon as my best chance of riding a winner on Dollar Seeker for Alan Bailey was in the next race. My horse jumped and travelled well underneath me and I cruised to the front at the third last. We swept into the straight and I was aware of a pursuer aiming to come on my inner. I edged towards the inside of the hurdle but it was all in vain as Dollar Seeker never took off properly and catapulted me out of the saddle. I lay curled up on the wet grass waiting for the quiet, feeling totally dejected. I wished for the ground to open and swallow me up and all the hurt would be no more... At the end of the week another good chance could only finish third at Ayr but it had been a change to stay with Stella Storey and her family for a week while I rode at three different northern tracks.

Howjal was a kookie, sulky character but, like most of those sorts, he just wanted a bit of attention, even if at times he laid his ears back at you. Sometimes he wanted to run away with you and sometimes he wouldn't want to go at all. I finished third on him at Fakenham and Ray Bostock and part owner Mick Rust were delighted, but on Boxing Day at Huntingdon in the cold and wet, *Howjal* was in a totally different mood. He missed the first hurdle and from then on I had a job to keep him interested and going; maybe he wasn't amused at me riding him out on Christmas morning! Declan Murphy was on board next time but he still didn't win. Fortunately I acquired a fan in Michael Whatley and rode his horse *Noble Rise* on a number of occasions. I tried as hard as I could to finish in the frame but the closest place was fifth. *Howjal* came good for me, though, and at the end of January we won an amateur hurdle on the all-weather track at Lingfield. Kitted out in stocking mask and two pairs of goggles (looking ready to rob a bank rather than ride a race) I had added protection when riding on this new surface. The kick-back from the oil-based mixture of shredded rubber and sand (Equitrack) was not pleasant when it hit you in the face and it was worse if you got a mouthful. But this was the least of my worries and I was so pleased to get my first winner over jumps since *Topori* at Fakenham in May 1988.

My return to Lingfield the following day to ride *Myliege* in a ladies' hurdle race on the turf was to be the first of many rides in February. Four days later I rode *Sobering Thoughts* in an all-weather flat race at the same track (an apt horse to ride as it was also my birthday) and then the very next day I travelled to Southwell to partner *Noble Rise* in an all-weather handicap hurdle. The all-weather racing was proving to be a good thing by keeping a lot of jockeys, flat and jumping, busy over the winter months when racing can often be abandoned due to the ground being frozen. The Southwell surface was fibresand and the kick-back was not quite as bad but we still wore the same protection. I was slightly disappointed when I finished second on *Howjal* to one of Martin Pipe's, as I felt that if I'd have kicked on sooner down the back straight, the outcome would have been different. Nobody else seemed to think that but I did. Riding regularly on the flat and over the jumps helped keep my mind off the emotional turmoil I was in. But it was still hard watching TC walk off in the opposite direction when racing had finished on those cold February nights.

I hardly missed a day riding out during those months and enjoyed teaching the youngsters as well as schooling the jumpers. David Thom told me to hop on a two-year-old he had in full breaking tack and on a lunge rein, to show a lad not to be afraid of using his legs on the young horse. He legged me up and I said there were no reins for me to hold. "You don't need reins," David smiled. After a few times round in a trot, David took the lunge rein off and told me to trot round controlling the horse myself. They all laughed after a couple circuits when I realised and suddenly said, "Gov'nor, I haven't got any reins!"

"I told you, you don't need reins!" he exclaimed. The lad thought we were all mad...

Riding out at Bostocks came slowly to an end by the end of February, although I still rode regular work on the heath at Newmarket when needed. Partnering *Aqiq* to finish second in a National Hunt flat race at Market Rasen was particularly pleasing. This son of *Shareef Dancer*, who we had nurtured over the winter months, looked quite promising. His rearing in playfulness had now all gone as he knuckled down to serious work. He was a lovely horse. Ray had started to use 7lb claimer John Towmey quite a lot by this time. A trainer always has to do the best he can and, although I was doing no wrong, it was a wise move to use this up-and-coming claimer on his horses in professional races. But I was particularly upset when Gerald Oxley rode *Howjal* at Fakenham on Amateur day. I still had three rides that day, though, and but for a bad blunder at the last hurdle, *Spanish Whisper*, who only failed by a neck, might have won. *Beechwood Cottage* ran his heart out in the two mile five hurdle and, although I had to pull up *Songbird Miracle*, all in all it wasn't a bad day. My jump season ended that day. I'd had twenty-five rides, a winner and six places. But I would never return home safe from a jump meeting again...

CHAPTER TEN

Give with One Hand

As the beginning of the flat season got underway, there was a minor thought about turning professional as I was now light enough to do 8st on the flat. It didn't mean that I would get any more rides, just be paid for them. I decided it was best for me to stay as an amateur, riding under both codes. I continued to scrutinise the papers every morning in hope of a few more jump rides, only ringing up for professional rides if I'd ridden the horse out at home for their trainer. I was riding out for David every day and the odd times at Alan's. Between them they gave me confidence and encouragement, helping me as much as they could, whenever they could.

My afternoon sessions riding out at David's had been on a two-year-old called *And Me*. We had spent many a cold February afternoon in the wilderness of an empty heath. I called her my *Baby Dolly Honkers* and it was a while before I realised that Alison Thom and Penny (who also worked for the Thoms) used to mimic me, but the three of us had a lot of fun and laughter riding out together. Now as the buds began to appear on the trees so did the numerous strings of horses. *Baby Doll* could whip round at the sight of a shadow ten yards away and Alison told me off for riding her so short. It didn't matter if she was ridden with a long length of stirrup or short – if she caught you unaware, mate, you were off! One day I hung precariously out of her right-hand side but fortunately gravity was with me and I managed to swing my left leg back where it should be. "I'm alright me." And another saying was born. I did fall off her a couple of times, and once when she was loose I called at her, "Baby Doll". They looked at me as if I was nuts but she came back and no one was more surprised than me.

Our breakfast time was after we had exercised two horses and were ready for one of David's culinary delights. From curries to casseroles there was nearly always something scrummy to eat and, if not, he'd buy an assortment of pies or rolls from the shop. We took it in turns to buy jars of honey, a different one each time, and sat there comparing them as if we were real connoisseurs while sipping on a packet-made cappuccino. I always left a crust for one of the Jack Russells. Robert was my favourite and he began to wait quite patiently for his treat, probably because he got a friendly kick if he tried to jump up at me. I'm not really a dog person but I liked Robert. On one occasion I was driving David to a night meeting and he asked me to be back by 12.30pm. I had done a few jobs for Alan and told him I had to shoot off as we were going racing. "You'll get there on a push bike, if you set off that early." It was one of his favourite sayings. We were having lunch first, I told him. "Lunch!" he exclaimed, "I'll have to tell Dave Thom not to spoil you." But he was pleased really...

One morning as I lingered in David's dining room after breakfast, scrutinising the entry form for the horses to be entered into amateur races, I heard the rattle of the wrought iron gate and was surprised when I looked up. "Alison," I exclaimed, "Lester Piggott's at the gate."

"OK," she replied.

"Alison, Lester Piggott's coming to the back door!"

"OK," she said, unperturbed. Alison opened the door and Lester went through to see David in the lounge. "Alison," I whispered, pointing to the door, "Lester Piggott's in your lounge." I hoped that David was arranging for the Maestro to come and ride a gallop and then I could ride upsides Lester Piggott, the man we all look up to and admire in our profession. Sadly, I never rode upsides Lester Piggott.

While having a chat one Sunday morning with my friend, Jennie, she asked if I had a ride in the Queen Mother's Cup. I told her I hadn't and she suggested I rang Henry Cecil – he might have something suitable and he did say he would have runners in ladies' races that year. I'd never asked a trainer I wasn't riding out for to run a horse for me, and told her so. "If you don't ring him, someone else will," she said. I thought about it for a while, about ten seconds, then rang Alan; he would tell me if I should. "Yes, give him a ring, Henry's alright," Alan assured me.

"I daren't," I replied pathetically, "will you ring him, for me?"

His reply was a definite "No". "He who dares wins, Murgy, he who dares wins!" A shaky hand dialled the number but there was no need to worry and, although Mr Cecil didn't have anything suitable for this particular race, he assured me of his intentions to run a few in ladies' races.

I met Alan over racecourse side to ride a two-year-old through the stalls. We laughed when I said I'd meet him over there, and he teased me, saying that I thought I was a jockey now. But I had not forgotten where I started and he had not forgotten that I'd worked for whatever I had. *Ever So Lonely* was by the same sire as *Call Up*, so she didn't have a lot going for her in my estimation. She had ability but was a bit backward in coming forward with it. I had recently ridden one that felt better for David. *Doesyoudoes* as in does-you-do or does-you-don't take Access, was named by him and had done everything that was asked of her. My support was stretched when both ran first time out at Warwick in the same race. The Thom team weighed in for their representative and the Baileys for theirs. I hung in suspended animation, wishing I didn't have to choose which one to cheer home. We backed *Doesyoudoes* at the very generous odds of 33/1 before it touched 20/1 ending up at 16/1, while *Ever So Lonely* was backed from 10/1 to 9/2. *Doesyoudoes* shot out of the stalls with *Ever So Lonely* taking time to find her stride, and at half way it looked like we would be collecting a tidy four figure sum. In the last few strides Alan Bailey's filly forced her head in front. And that's racing...

If I thought *Howjal* was kookie, then I hadn't bargained on meeting *Norfolk Lady*. We nicknamed her "*Angie Baby*" after the song by Helen Reddy, about a schizophrenic girl living in a world of make-believe. As my old boss, Tony Dickinson, would say, she definitely had a slate loose! For me the almost black filly with one white rimmed eye was a challenge for my riding skills. As long as she was mounted in the stable and kept moving forward on the heath she was fine... Although some wouldn't agree. Unfortunately, this was not always possible and it was me who broke down the plastic trotting rails on racecourse side when she suddenly ploughed through them. After the damage was done she calmly turned and trotted back to the others. Strange. The first time she ran as a three-year-old she half reared, half fell over in the paddock with Stuart Webster. Maybe David was only joking when he said "she runs in a ladies' race next." But as the joke was now, everytime I patted one on the neck, I put my name down for it to ride in a race!

And here I was on the road to Kempton to ride her. Too much chat and not enough concentration with my friend Joss and I'd taken a wrong turn. My mini metro screamed at me as my foot stayed flat to the boards back up the M25 heading for Kempton's 6.30pm ladies' race. "I don't think you're meant to drive these cars this fast," Joss said, knuckles white, holding onto the edge of the seat. Meanwhile, as it approached 5.45pm and still no sign of me, owner and trainer were becoming slightly worried. David was adamant: there would be no jockey change much to the owner's dismay. If I did not arrive in time she would have to be withdrawn. It would not be fair for someone who didn't know what she was like to ride her, even those who offered. Terry and Wendy Jennings who owned her understood. They are good horse people.

I arrived in the nick of time and, as I'd already arranged to borrow a saddle from Jimmy Quinn, I quickly changed and weighed out. We had permission to mount a little earlier than the others and, while Janet Boston led and kept *Angie* on the move, David legged me on. This all went okay but she stopped just outside the paddock and began to back up. I still didn't have my feet in the irons but I was confident that she wouldn't gallop off with me if I did manage to get her away from the tree she was now brushed up against. David shouted at me to "get off her". He felt that what ability we thought she might have was not worth anybody being injured over. I gave her a heavy boot in the ribs and she shot forward into canter and in the right direction. Once past the stands, ready to turn and canter back towards the starting gate, I cursed Jimmy Quinn. He told me the stirrup leathers would be long enough for me but when I placed my feet in the irons, I was riding as short as Lester Piggott. I suppose he was getting his own back for all the hard work I made him do when we worked at Alan Bailey's yard!

I rode her twice more, at Redcar where that year the Redcar/Lingfield day was achieved by aeroplane, Teesside to Gatwick. I looked forward to riding *Jet Pet*, *Jedders*, at Lingfield as he was one of my favourites and, with lifts arranged at both ends, we sat back to the best afternoon tea David and I had ever had. I was legged up onto *Angie* on the course at Redcar just as she decided to leap forward, and I slid off landing on my feet. But the funniest time on reflection was at Doncaster. She did her usual bobbing about while I was put in the saddle and I cantered her half way down to post with no irons, as usual. She behaved herself impeccably as I walked her up and down at the start but the next minute, when there was only myself and another to be put in stall, Tanya Bracegirdle's horse leapt forward hitting mine on the backside. I, unaware until impact, shot out of the side door (her left-hand side). Luckily I kept hold of the reins as I quickly rose to my feet and she looked at me, even more astonished than ever. There was a big problem now. Without my trainer and owner to leg me back into the saddle, I'd have to hope she would be alright when a stall handler tried. There was no way, as she half reared twice. They put her in the stalls without me, at my suggestion, and all I had to do was get up onto the stalls and climb over onto her back. It worked a treat after I embarrassingly asked for a lift onto the stalls to start with! She never ran again, after showing nothing, but I did want to ride her in the Ripon Ladies' Derby over a mile and a half, only she was balloted out.

Amidst the riding out and racing there was little time for socialising – not that I was in the least bit bothered. A quiet supper with Joss, Ali and Gov (David Thom) or Jennie and Bryn or a trip out to the Linden Tree at Bury was often pleasant and often harrowing. I wasn't too rapt about going to the Cambridge midsummer fair but, as there were two couples going, Ali and I decided we might as well go, even if it was just for the candyfloss. I'd been once before, of course, but I tried not to think about that. Gypsy Rose Lee had me handing over a tenner to look in the crystal ball before I stepped into the caravan. The spiel was so well rehearsed and being told so many things in such a short space of time was both believable and unbelievable. The upshot of my tenner's worth was not that I would meet a rich and handsome man, become champion lady jockey and live happily ever after. When Alison asked me the foretelling I told her with distaste and annoyance at handing over the money, "She thought I was a bloody nurse, she could see me surrounded by nurses!"

After riding out one sunny June Sunday morning I returned home to find a message on the answerphone. I had waited in anticipation for this call and I dialled Mr Cecil's number before I drew breath. He wanted me to ride *Grammos*, owned by Mr Marinopoulos, at Kempton a week Wednesday. I was delighted, absolutely delighted. My next call was to Alan Bailey and then David to share my news. How my life had changed in the previous eight months. Riding for Cecil is like Williams-Renault is to a racing driver. The Diamonds might not elude me for very much longer, but I still felt the devastation of loneliness and would have gladly traded them in.

It was another a sunny day when I set out to drive north back to Gisburn. The small church was packed to capacity for us to say our goodbyes to the man we had called the Boss. The occasion brought a lot of old acquaintances and friends together and I knew he was proud of all our achievements. Michael Dickinson and Mrs D thanked us for coming, but it was us who were the thankful ones.

I couldn't help feeling a little smug as I drove up the road to Warren Place for my first ride out on *Grammos*. "Be here at seven for coffee," Mr Cecil had said the previous day and David said, "you'll still have time to ride out one here before you go." This worked out really well and when I started to ride out twice a week I was still back at David's in time for breakfast! From that first day I was made to feel welcome and there did not seem to be any animosity. They were a great bunch of lads and girls and I fitted in well. Willie Ryan, who is stable jockey, was particularly helpful and told me not to expect too much from *Grammos*, and he proved to be right. *Grammos* could only finish second at Kempton to *Suserration*, which was trained by John Gosden and ridden by Lydia Pearce. The soft ground was a hindrance more than a help.

I was disappointed but Mr Cecil just shrugged it off, "Don't worry, you've got another ride next week." At the end of June all amateurs renew their riding licences. I was surprised when I counted that I'd had fifty-eight rides in the past twelve months and hoped to kick off with a winner on my new one. *Snickersnee* didn't have any sort of form and had been just about tailed off at Newmarket on his previous run. He was a big, kind horse, and very laid back. Some of the lads laughed when they knew I was riding him at Yarmouth, saying, "you will have to be fit to ride that!" The sea fret came down quickly and, although the spectators could not see us until the final two furlongs, visibility was not too bad. I sat in third and got a great run up the inner turning into the straight and *Snickers* did the rest to record my first win of the season. David was the first to congratulate me, even though he had a runner in the race. I had ridden a winner for Henry Cecil and it felt brilliant. The only down side was returning to an empty house, and I wished so hard I could stop feeling this way.

At the end of May I had rung up for the ride on a horse called *The Right Time* for John Parkes. He had run well, finishing third at Redcar, but I knew as soon as the race was over I'd hit the front too soon. Mr Parkes had him down to run at Edinburgh and I rode him again, this time doing a little better, finishing second. As was normal practice the Newmarket jockeys used to drive to Peterborough railway station where they would board the 9am train to Edinburgh; Epsom jockeys had already got on at King's Cross. We then travelled up country for the Malton-based jockeys to board at York. We arrived in Edinburgh and got a taxi to the racecourse which took about fifteen minutes, only three-quarters of an hour to spare before our race at 2pm. After the race there was little time to rest on our laurels, with the taxi already booked for the lady jockeys at 3.30pm in time to catch the departing 4pm train, arriving back at Peterborough at 7.38pm. None of us wanted to be too late home and there was still a forty-five minute drive back to Newmarket for me. That year Elaine Bronson got on at King's Cross, and Anthea Farrell at York, and the journey was far from boring.

My second winner of the season put me into close third place in the Championship behind Elaine and Clare Balding. Elaine had had four winners and I now was only eleven points behind her. My weekend win was far removed from what I had been used to. David Furlong, who had owned *Rose Glen* before this run (she was now owned by a racing syndicate called Laurel Leisure), drove myself and Alan Bailey to Ayr on Friday ready for the race at the Scottish track the next day. I felt like the Queen as I sat in the back of the big Mercedes watching the scenery go by. It was the English summer at its best. I had plenty of time to go for a long run on the beach before meeting for dinner and afterwards I sat for a while watching the waves and the sea stretching out to nowhere in particular. I thought about a poem I had written called "Racing Day Runaways", while working for the Dickinsons. I had become friendly with a lad from Neville Crump's stable called John, who looked after a good horse called *Even Melody*. We only ever saw each other when we were racing, which wasn't very often. I tried so hard to remember the verse but the only lines I could recall were, "we walked and talked as the sea blew in sand and salt and the wind carried our laughter away on that cold and biting racing day." It was funny to think that thirteen years ago I had walked along this beach so young and carefree. Yet now, even with most ambitions fulfilled and comfortable with my way of life, which was really problem free, I felt sad...

The following day I spoiled myself by making use of the hotel facilities. I arrived at the races relaxed and in a much better frame of mind. Lydia was quite envious when I told her I had spent the morning languishing in a jacuzzi after a sauna, sunbed and swimming session! Now all I had to do was ride a winner. I hit the front on *Rose Glen* two furlongs out and, although Lydia came within a length of me, I was always confident of winning. I was thrilled for Alan; it was another reminder of how well he could train while trying so hard to keep his head above water. I had ridden my first winner for him and, as it turned out, I had just ridden my last...

It was 9.45pm when David Furlong dropped me off at home and I rang my friend Joss as we had arranged to meet up if I wasn't too late. Her boyfriend, Richard Levin, and some of his London friends had been racing and were going to finish the night off at the newly opened Dance Hall. My mind and body did not want to sleep just yet, still running off the adrenalin of the day, so I was eager to find them. Joss had decided to give the dancing a miss so we went to the Moat House Hotel in Newmarket, staying there chatting until 2am. I valued our friendship and I think we both felt good after our long chat. We were very fortunate.

I was thrilled to see a Cecil runner in the amateur race on Thursday evening as I sat in my car looking through the entries outside the paper shop at 5am on Monday, fresh from my latest victory and already looking forward to the next. Mr Cecil had told me that I would ride *Grammos* in the Diamond race, which was the following Saturday, but when I went to ride him out the next day, I was pointed in the direction of the Thursday runner. I clenched my fist in delight as I made my way over to *Friedland*'s stable and was even more excited to see he was owned by Sheikh Mohammed. After a swinging canter on the Limekilns Mr Cecil said he would run on Thursday and I could ride *Snickersnee* a gallop the next day to keep my lungs clear! I smiled to myself, thinking his were the last horses I needed to be fit for and, as I stroked *Friedland* down his neck, he was definitely a Ferrari next to most I had ridden. I dashed back to Exning bursting with my news and wasted no time ringing up the press to put my name down for him. Mr Cecil was quite apologetic in the morning when he told me that I could not ride *Friedland* as Lucinda Stopford Sackville, who had ridden for Sheikh Mohammed before and was still looking for her first win, was riding him. I was disappointed, yes, but it was far from the end of the world, there were plenty of rich pickings still to be had. I told her he was a lovely horse and to go and ride herself a winner. A few of the lads tried to get to me saying "got the jock, then?"

"Yes it's tough at the top," I smiled. This was just another minor setback which I had already learnt to cope with. No one ever knows what waits for them around the corner of fate and *Friedland* was the only winner Lucinda rode on the flat; she had a fatal car crash in December '93.

We looked set to meet Lydia on *Suserration* again and hoped to turn the tables on the faster ground in the Diamond race at Ascot. It was not to be; any glimmer of hope soon faded as we swung into the straight right on the heels of *Suserration* but under pressure. Upsides my great pal, Jennie Crossley, riding in the apricot colours of Lord Howard de Walden for Julie Cecil; we had come a long way from our humble beginnings. Champagne was already chilling in the changing room sink – win, lose or draw we had decided this Diamond day would be etched on our minds forever.

It was right and fitting that Lydia won the Diamonds, and a group of us who had changed together were pleased we had anticipated the result. The champagne was chilled and, as it tickled the back of our throats, we laughed and giggled. Some would say, we were like silly schoolgirls but I would say we were pleased to share Lydia's moment of glory, hoping that next year it would be one of us! As Jennie and I modelled our Marks and Spencer's underwear, Elaine Bronson was more intent on opening the first bottle, ready to spray Lydia in true racing car fashion, but Lyd took so long to appear we had to drink the first bottle without her! Finally she appeared to a quick spray of champagne (we didn't want to waste too much) and plenty of genuine cheering. It was an absolutely marvellous day and I was glad my friend Joss and her sister Alex had come with me – and not only because Joss could drive home, as I ended the day quite inebriated. Unfortunately this led to me falling into a satisfying sleep and when Joss nudged me to ask, "Is it this way round the M25?" I mistakenly said, "Yes," only half awake. I was not popular when we eventually arrived home to Newmarket. Fresh as a daisy, I asked, "Where have we to head for tonight, girls?" But my two tired travelling companions were by now in no mood to party, the journey taking much longer than it should have...

My loyal friends were, by now, quite fed up with my bleating on about a broken heart, but they never really showed it. They pointed out how lucky I was and how much I had going for me. I would soon meet someone and TC would be a distant memory again, gone but never forgotten. I wanted to be home when I was out and out when I was home. My lodgers, whom I had acquired over the last couple of months, seemed to be taking over the house. Sometimes I didn't mind and other times I wished they would just disappear.

My roller-coaster emotions were uncontrollable, ruled by seeing TC and by the events of my career. I was feeling pretty pleased with myself when I rang the press to put my name down to ride *Independent Air* at Bangor, before flying to Beverley to ride *Smoke* in a ladies' flat race for John Parkes, on Tuesday July 30th 1991. I fairly sparkled with a healthy suntan and fitness, so when I saw TC later that morning I was definitely on a high. I might as well have been on the moon. "Why?" I asked, but there was no answer. I will survive, I told myself, no matter how long it takes; I will survive!

None of my fellow jockeys flying to Beverley in the six-seater plane wanted to sit next to the pilot. Richard Hills, Willie Ryan, Carole Wall and Jennie soon hopped in the back. I'm not sure what the pilot thought as I asked about every dial and instrument that covered the panel in front of us. I kept turning to Jennie to tell her the latest details of the flight: "We're flying at 5000 feet and still climbing!" The pilot radioed ahead, as we needed a taxi from the airfield to the track, and it was waiting when we landed. Even my earlier confrontation could not dampen the enthusiasm for my first flight from Newmarket to the races and, by the start of our race, everyone on Beverley racecourse knew my transport had wings. Once changed, my lady colleagues and I were ready to do battle again but you wouldn't have thought so judging by the way Elaine, Jennie and myself sprawled out, leaning against each other on the changing room settee. Black polished boots resting on an old coffee table were tapped unceremoniously by our whips. We were relaxed and laid back but ready to jump into action at a moment's notice. Our camaraderie was second to none. David Wilson, trainer of *Cathos*, Elaine's mount, did not quite see it like that and scolded us for not appearing more alert.

As soon as the stalls opened our alertness was in no doubt. I tracked to the inside rail on *Smoke*, from a wide draw, to sit handy upsides Annie Usher and Elaine. Jennie ranged up on my outside and as she went into second, I, with enough room, cut in and went third. Elaine and Annie screamed at me for taking their ground – it may have been a bit tight but that's race riding. As we all turned into the straight, I marvelled at the tremendous run I was having out of the grey mare. But no sooner had I gone to take the lead than Elaine appeared on *Cathos*. Setting my mare alight I tried to pinch a length but *Cathos* extended to go a couple of lengths clear as we ran to the furlong pole and I would have to settle for second. Elaine, confident that the race was in the bag, stopped pushing her horse, looking over her left shoulder for any other dangers so she could ease him down to the line. *Smoke* was in no mood to accept defeat without a fight and neither was I and, whilst Elaine looked left again, we made ground quickly up the inside rail only failing by a neck! It was a terrific race and, if I'd have got up to beat her, she would never have heard the last of it. As it was she was very pleased.

I piloted the plane for about five minutes on the way home. This time I told Jennie, "I'm flying you over the River Humber." She's not usually too bad in flight but seemed a bit shaky then for some reason! The pilot was a bit concerned about my big dipper route and politely said he had better take full control or Willie Ryan would not get to Leicester in time for the evening racing. I was not to know that my next flight to Newmarket would be in a helicopter – after being surrounded by nurses, as the fortune teller had predicted...

It was a hive of activity next morning on the schooling links. Sean Woods was schooling a filly for Alan Bailey and I was giving *Jedders* and *The Grey Job* a final school before deciding which one to ride at Bangor on Friday. David Thom made me feel really important in front of the on-lookers; I was his jockey, I had done the ground work and I would ride in the race...

Give with One Hand
and Take Away with Two

OoO

And now, God, what am I to do?
You gave to me with one hand
And take away with two
I know you see me fighting
But how strong are you?
To give me happiness with one hand
And then take it away with two

When snow fell so cold was I
You took my love away
I thought that I would die
With both hands you dragged him away
He said no love... could not stay
You gave him to me long enough
For me to love and treasure
You gave to me with one hand
And took away my love and life with another

But did you see me try so hard
To find my life?
And now when things are going well
You do it to me again!
But you have made me stronger
My Lord, stronger... than you will ever know
Because as I take with one hand
For luck... I'll take a little more
Just in case some more unhappiness
For me is waiting by the door
Then sometimes in my sadness
You will come along
Maybe to give to me with two hands
And never to take away with one

OoO

Sharron Murgatroyd

CHAPTER ELEVEN

Take Away with Two

I never saw "the light" that I'd heard people describe and I never thought I would die. I was very sleepy and not really perturbed by what the doctor had said. But there would be times during the next seven months when I would wish I had just slipped away where I lay on the warm turf in the furore of the racecourse, with the heat of the shining sun and in the midst of my beloved sport. No more hurting, no more heartache, no more pretending. An easy way out for me. Maybe... because I would feel so guilty when I saw the torment and utter devastation in my mother's face and the bewilderment at what was happening in my brothers' and sister's. And then there was my father who I felt, however hard he tried, would never be able to make amends for the neglect of the past. But fate had decided to give me another challenge. The chance to live and breathe again.

I was still being examined by doctors when my mum, brother Clive and his wife, Bonita, arrived. I was so tired and the doctor kept on and on asking me questions. Every so often I'd feel the sharp prick of a needle on my face or shoulder, on my neck and ear. And then there was the voice of the doctor asking me what I could feel. They were doing the same thing over and over again, asking the same questions. I was becoming increasingly annoyed and agitated with the queries. It was midnight by the time my mum saw me. She had been informed by Wrexham's Maelor hospital of my accident and that it was a spinal injury. I was being transferred by ambulance to Oswestry but it would only travel at ten miles an hour so it would be some time before I arrived there. "You shouldn't have come all this way," I told her, "I'm alright." To me she didn't look too upset but she was distraught with worry even before she was aware of the full implications. The doctor told her after I'd had my scan that I had broken my neck very badly and my body was paralysed. It would be six weeks before all the bleeding and swelling around the damaged area had subsided and they could diagnose the full extent of my injury. Although I was quite stable my condition was critical. She would have to be very brave. She prayed for me to hang onto life, just like she had done seventeen months earlier for my brother Mark when he had fractured his skull playing football. After his scan the surgeons had found it necessary to operate. During a five hour operation to mend tissues that cover the brain they were astonished to find and remove a piece of bone that had lodged in his brain and had to insert a metal plate to stabilise his forehead. He recovered fully but could never play football again.

When I woke up on Saturday morning I knew I was in hospital, I knew

I couldn't move my arms or legs and I knew it was my own fault... I wondered who would be riding *Snickersnee* at Newmarket. Bollocks, I thought, bloody bollocks! A nurse appeared. "How are you this morning?" She was light and breezy and I liked that. She checked the drip that was taped into my right hand and stuck a thermometer in my mouth, just as I'd said, "Fine thank you, how are you?" My voice was still little more than a whisper and I was surprised at how tight my chest was and how numb my body felt. I asked if my mum was still there. She had gone home but was coming back today. I didn't hurt anywhere but I couldn't move my head. It felt really heavy. I remembered what the doctor had said, something about six weeks before the swelling would go down. Yeah, I thought, I'll be alright then, my apparent alertness and clear head clicking into positive mode. At the beginning you cannot begin to realise what has happened to you. My body that had been doing all the work needed a rest, it would be all back to normal soon. And if it isn't? I asked myself. Well I knew this could happen; every jockey knows the risks involved. I would have to face it and fight it and, while still feeling hurt and neglected at having my heart torn apart, this new situation seemed secondary.

Parents or spouses were encouraged to stay for the first few weeks if it was possible. There was accommodation laid on and the "Lodge" must be witness to many a heartbroken mother, father, wife or husband. I was lucky my mum could have time off work, and she helped to nurse me for the first seven weeks while I was confined to bed. We were to live through some times in those weeks that we could never have envisaged.

She was shocked to see me in head traction when she returned; laid in a crucifix position on a high tilting bed. The metal stabilisers (callipers) were fixed into the skull about three-quarters of an inch above the ears, crossed over in a scissor action, and my head felt heavy because of the seven pounds of iron weight that hung off them and down the back of the bed. I'd had a fairly comfortable night, what was left of it, and only needed the oxygen mask intermittently. She was requested to answer the ward phone the first couple of days, as it rang constantly with inquiries about me. I was overwhelmed by the amount of calls that were made from friends and the racing fraternity.

As is the norm in this type of injury, the two-hour check of temperature is vital. A rise or fall of temperature, which the body has difficulty in controlling, is life threatening. I was rushed into the resuscitation room (hot house) on Sunday afternoon when my temperature had fallen way below normal. Covered in lots of blankets and a foil sheet, I came to and thought they were trying to cook me. My head felt like it was going to explode, and I could feel my cheeks pumping as if I'd been running and sweating. I was glad to see my mum and Vicky Jones (trainer's daughter from Oswestry) and told them to "get me out of this hot house!" I couldn't breathe and could hardly get the words out as the tightness in my chest seemed to move up around my throat. Panic set in – to patient, young nurse, mum and Vicky. The sister who arrived on duty soon took charge of the situation and had me out of the hot house and back on the ward. That was the second problem of my eventful day. Earlier that morning, when I'd had difficulty in breathing, I was fitted with an oxygen mask and told to take long slow breaths but nothing was happening. There seemed to be a block in the tube, so Sister Linda quickly changed the cylinder but it still wasn't working. She replaced the mask with a nasal oxygen intake but the drips of water that are supposed to keep the passages moist were running down my throat, nearly drowning me! The actual problem was the connection to the oxygen cylinder. Once that was replaced everything calmed down.

The next couple of days were spent drifting in and out of sleep. I seemed to be wide awake all through the night except when I needed to be turned in the bed, which was done every three hours to avoid pressure on the skin. Then through the day I was either alert and coming out with all sorts of profound messages to well wishers or sleeping happily on cloud nine with a big smile on my face. "There's someone here to see you," my mum's voice said; I opened my eyes and was pleased to see TC standing there. His face was ashen and I told him not to worry, I'd be alright. I knew I would have to be strong where he was concerned and, however hard I'd taken the break-up until now, it would get a lot worse before it began to get better...

It would be a while before the dreams, reality and disorientation that were mixing up settled down and I languished in my hospital bed making jokes and laughing so much that I became short of breath and was repeatedly told to behave myself. I hadn't had a lie in for months I told the nurses! My broken heart hurts more than a broken neck and when can I have my legs waxed? I told my mum to go and buy presents for every one of my friends; but, thank goodness, she didn't! I inquired into every tablet that was prescribed, wanting to know what they were for and refusing pain killers; I had no pain. "I'm just giving you an injection in your thigh," the nurse would say and I would reply, "Okay." I relayed statements to all and sundry, reliving my accident as if I'd won a Gold Cup. My behaviour and attitude to what had happened was being controlled by the pain-killing injection that was sunk into my unfeeling thigh at regular intervals. The daily reports in the trade papers and being inundated with cards and flowers was unbelievable and proved to be my strength. I couldn't let anybody down by admitting defeat. I felt that it was down to me. I would have to pull my family, friends and anyone else who had been touched by my misfortune, through these times. I would try not to whimper, I would try not to say, "Why me?" I would try to show the spirit and determination of the many brave horses I had ridden.

So while I pushed the threat of never walking again away, I faced my visitors with a smile, hoping to put them at ease. It was as hard for my friends to walk into that ward as it was for me knowing I might never walk out. The emotions shown by my close friends Alan and Jan Bailey, Jennie and Bryn Crossley, Joss Drake, and especially David and Alison Thom were all so different but meant just as much. All of us were reminded of the powers of success and the extremes of danger in our sport, where the glory and tears lay side by side.

I asked to see my x-rays which were produced by one of the doctors who told me I'd be up and about in no time, pointing to a faint crack in the vertebrae that could be seen on the black perspex picture of a skeleton neck... The vertebrae are the bones which encase the spinal column and inside the column there are millions of nerves which, when given commands by the brain, make our bodies move, feel and sense. Our body is an intricate piece of machinery and every vertebra part is numbered by doctors – from the base of the skull (C1) to just above the tail bone. So some of the nerves or all of the nerves can be severed or stretched by broken vertebrae, thus stopping the flow of instructions for movement, sensation and feeling. I had already been well informed about the damage I'd done to my neck. Hitting the ground at such force with my head in flexion (bent forward) I had managed to break five vertebrae and crush one into dust. C3 was the first vertebrae to be damaged and splinters of bone had penetrated at C4, C5, and C6; C7 was just about non-existent and T1 (first in the back) was cracked too. The doctor apologised profusely when I said, "I think you have someone else's x-rays, doctor."

I soon picked-up the hospital jargon; they did not always agree but I made the nurses and sometimes the doctors laugh with my interpretation of the statements. For instance, "her family are at her bedside," really means, "she could go at any minute!" "Sharron remains comfortable." It took me a while to get this one, well I did skip school, but I should have known that it meant, "Sharron is stuck to the ceiling due to one in the leg." I can understand how people can beg, steal or borrow for drugs. I didn't quite realise, until I had to come off the high powered 0.3ml Temgesic drug, exactly what it did for me but fourteen days later I knew my holiday was over. Beautiful dreams, thoughts and feelings left my mind and body. My peaceful easy life snuggling into the soft clouds, being caressed lovingly again and making me strong mentally, until I recovered, were gone. I was quite jittery by late morning and it was unfortunate that Brendan Powell and Ray Bostock saw me becoming distressed. But not as unfortunate as if they had witnessed me become quite hysterical as the effects of the drug completely wore off by late afternoon. Every part of my body was racked with an intense burning and stinging pain, especially my arms. I thought I was losing what little feeling I had in my arms. I shouted at the nurses for something, anything to make it stop! My mum tried to comfort me by saying that TC and Brendan had been to see me, she didn't know what to do or say. I turned everything round into horror, "They only came 'cause they think I'm going to die!" I retorted. The curtains were round the bed trying to muffle my words of abuse directed at everyone, present or not... So this is "cold turkey!"

One of the doctors was called; he would later earn the title Dr Personality. He asked me "What's wrong?" a question that at any other time would have been answered with, "Well, apart from a broken neck, being paralysed and hurting all over, I've just got this excruciating pain in my arms, so I was wondering, you being a doctor and all, if there was anything you could do to make my misery a little more bearable." But I had become too distressed by this time and the shock horror on my mum and brother Mark's faces was a reminder of what I was putting them through. I told him of the pain in my arms and he made me comfortable for the last time with the leg injection. The next time I was offered pain killers, there was no hesitation.

With pain killers and sleeping tablets last thing at night it is no wonder that the dreams were weird and wonderful, albeit a little distressing at times. Waking up with the realisation of being unable to move, after dreaming of running barefoot through green fields, the summer breeze softly blowing your hair and lots of laughter, was a shade cruel even by my standards but it was better than the times when I woke up feeling like a corkscrew. "Nurse, why do I feel like a corkscrew?" I'd ask and they would say, "Is this another joke?" This time it wasn't. I felt as if my body was twisting round and round from the neck down. An old scar right in the middle of the back of my head proved to be a horrendous pressure point. The only relief was for a nurse to take the weight of my head off the piece of foam with its cut out circle that served as a pillow. This could only be done by the fully trained nurses and there wasn't always one available.

I was moved down the ward away from the office to make room for other unfortunate victims. I had Richard from Somerset on one side and Richard the biker from wherever on the other. Richard from Somerset had been driving his van down the motorway when for some reason he hit a bridge. He had broken his neck. Richard the biker met his misfortune under very mysterious circumstances and had broken his back. His visitors were often five or six of the biggest and hairiest leather clad rockers you could ever wish to meet. One night I heard him saying to one of them, "don't worry about me, mate, I'll be out of here by the end of the week, I feel great," and I thought to myself, that's the best stuff he has ever been on! We all struck up a sort of friendship in the first few weeks and, although unable to see each other, we could recognise one another's voices – mine being the easiest as I was the only female in the ward for some time.

We were all experiencing the same thing but it affected us differently. And we handled it differently too – sometimes with laughter, sometimes with a very positive attitude and sometimes with the contempt it deserved. I told the nurse I was cold. The thermometer read I had a raging temperature. The windows were flung open and I was stripped of bed covers and wrapped in cold wet towels. I trembled with the fever. This cannot be real, I thought to myself. What else can happen and how much can I take?... How much can any of us take?

The order of the day was, after a 5.00am turn, breakfast and painkillers at 7.00am, and then the nurses would go into the office for the report. This was day staff taking over from night staff. For twenty minutes you couldn't get a nurse for love nor money and while my mum was there she ended up fetching and carrying for everyone. "Mrs Murgatroyd, are you there? It's Peter, could you pass me a drink please?" and she would reply, "Course I can love," and I would say, "Get your own bloody mother!" It would make them giggle. I was very lucky because my mum came in to give me breakfast and I could recognise her footsteps as she turned into the ward every morning. We would often talk of our accidents at this time and it would start with "Morning, Sharron" and then I'd say "Morning, Richard" then someone else would say "Morning, Peter", "Morning, John", "Morning, Steve", "Morning, Sharron", "Morning, Darren" (who had over his bed "I'm too sexy for this bed"). John, who had been a milkman, used to say, "I'd be delivering my milk now to her at number 10. I can just see her in that see-through negligee – she didn't half fancy me," and the other boys used to jeer, telling him he was dreaming. Some of the stories were horrific and some were quite funny. "What happened to you then, John?" someone asked and the story was: on a sunny day out at Rhyl he and three friends were diving into the sea. Unfortunately, John dived in as the waves were going out and hit his head on the seabed. To liven his story up (as most of us did) he said his friends just sat on the beach drinking beer and eating sandwiches, not worrying about him. Some who had been in car accidents could not remember much, and some swore they saw a light shining brightly but a voice told them it was not time yet or a hand waved them back. I told them that I felt robbed; I hadn't seen anything and wondered if theirs were mere fabrication.

The nurses would then bustle into action, with the sound of curtains swishing on rails, water sloshing in bowls and lively chatter as everyone was washed from head to toe. The nurses admired my brown slim body and told me to make sure I was creamed with body lotion every day; it would not keep me brown or slim but it would help to keep my skin from getting rough and sore. I asked them to keep me as covered up as they could (they respected my wishes) as I tried to hold on to my dignity as much as I could. They might have had a laugh about it but they could laugh all they liked as long as I wasn't left half naked for all to see at the twitch of a curtain. The curtains swished open one morning, two nurses appeared and a man. "This is male nurse, Brian," one of them said.

"Hello Brian, goodbye Brian," I said casually. There were all these men in the ward and they had sent Brian in to help wash me, if you please. I shook my head in disbelief.

The cards, letters and flowers were the next things to be sorted out. The words of hope and inspiration from so many kind people who took the time to think about me were overwhelming. A prayer sent on a betting slip came from Ireland, as did a present of a religious Scapular. It seemed a shame to throw away the wilted flowers and my mum shredded the petals off the stems and dried nearly a bin liner full. I had an idea that pot pourri could be made; it worked and I have a wicker basket full, thanks to my mum.

I would often feel quite tired at this time and I could have had a bet that as soon as I drifted into sleep I would be woken up by one of the physios. Pat would come to move my arms and legs. It was all so gentle now but I was warned that they would become pretty ruthless when I started to go into the gym. One particular morning when I was settling down and listening to my favourite Chris Rea tape, Pat appeared. She moved my legs first, bending toes and ankles in all directions and we chatted about all sorts of things. She moved my arms and left them bent and raised above my head, resting on the pillow, and told me to ask a nurse to move them back into the normal crucifix position after about ten minutes. This would ensure that all my arm muscles would have a good stretch. "OK," I said and asked her to switch my walkman back on. I woke up half an hour later... "Nurse!" I screamed and, when one appeared, I asked her, "where's my arms?" I could not see them and certainly couldn't feel them, not, that is until she began to move them down. "You can't hurt me," I lied, "I'm a jump jockey!"

Visiting was from 12 noon until 8pm but sometimes some of the lads that were overnight racing at Chester from Newmarket would turn up as early as 10.30am. "It won't happen again," I promised and just hoped different staff would be on if it did! I was pleasantly surprised day after day at the people who made the effort to come and see me. There were some I knew, some I hardly knew and some I didn't know at all.

It was a pity that it took something like this to happen for me to spend time with my sister, Justine. We hadn't shared a lot of the sister sort of stuff as she was only a kid when I was going through my adolescence and then, as she pointed out, I left home when she was nine. We had gone our different ways, not needing each other for advice or support, but we knew it was there if we did. Sometimes we had not got on very well since I'd moved away. With her grown up and the same strength of character, nobody was going to dictate to her, but we did have some fun times. She now sat by my bedside peeling and feeding me grapes. "I never thought I'd do this for you," she said. She had a week off work and stayed at the Jones' so she could see me every day. I had interrupted my brothers' and sister's lives with all the trailing up and down the motorway from Yorkshire, the journey taking a good three hours if the roads were clear. I was aware of this and hoped that I wouldn't be a burden for too long.

Even though my head had been unaffected by the fall (I think), my helmet most definitely saving me from extinction, some normal reactions were slow to return until the shock started to lift. All of a sudden I realised I was blinking and although the diaphragm was unable to push enough air into my lungs for a sneeze or cough, my voice had become a little stronger. Four weeks had gone by and although I could raise my left arm up onto my elbow for a few seconds, the prognosis was not good. It was this new movement that made me over optimistic that all faculties would return. Dr El Masry in his wisdom felt it was time to tell me the drastic news; there was no point in waiting the full six weeks until all the swelling had gone down. The damage was irreversible; I would never regain full use of my limbs. In time I would strengthen and have upper arm movement. My left arm would be quite mobile and it was possible that I might be able to feed myself and brush my teeth, with certain aids, but I would never have normal working hands again. The right arm should also find a range of movement but the impact of crushed bone had affected that side worst. I would never be able to wash or dress myself and I would never be able to style my hair. "Lucky I don't need make-up then." I half smiled at the doctor but couldn't look at my mum. I was thirty-one years old and would spend the rest of my life in a wheelchair. "No more race riding," I thought, as if that would be the only thing I would miss. How wrong I was; time would tell me of the many menial things that would become much more important. "But, you are young and strong and will still be able to live a life," said Dr El Masry. And why shouldn't I!

I respected and believed Dr El Masry. I also liked him but it did not stop me doubting his final analysis. My x-rays were sent to a Dr Kerlin in America. He was a friend of Sir Charles Wacker III who owned *Snickersnee* and had seen Bill Shoemaker (Champion American jockey) after a bad car accident that had left him paralysed by a spinal cord injury. Even though he agreed with all that had been said, at times I would still think that I could be "the miracle baby". The pressure from people who are trying so hard to be helpful is overpowering and all of a sudden, they know more than the doctors. But what is more overpowering is that you start to believe them. "If you are really strong, you WILL walk again." "Never give up hope." "Doctors are always getting it wrong." All this adds to the trauma, I suppose, and sometimes I didn't know if I was on my head or my arse. So I repeated what everyone was telling me. The headlines read, "Sharron to prove doctors wrong" and "I will walk and ride again." But it was rubbish and I wish I'd never said anything.

I also put on this fighting talk for the benefit of the lady and male jockeys who came to see me. I couldn't let Candy Morris or Lorna Vincent or my rival buddy Elaine Bronson think that I would ever give in. Even more so TC and, when they were all around my bed, it seemed impossible to me that I would not soon be joining them at "the start".

The head callipers came off as promised after six weeks. I had been very wicked telling visitors that doctors had drilled them in with a Black and Decker! Dr Personality came along with his screwdriver and, after removing the weights, there was a short twang and then they were off. I would be able to have a shower now but it wasn't as nice as I thought it would be. The next day I was transferred onto a plastic shower trolley and wheeled off into the bathroom. It was like being in the car wash but at least I got my hair washed. I couldn't wait to sit up and was very disappointed when the next day I was raised only 20 degrees by my nurse Julie. But I persuaded her to put me up another 20 – at least I would then be able to see something. By this time I shared the ward with fifteen men (not that pleasant I can assure you), and had the bed on its own at the far end of the ward. It was very different to how I imagined it to be. I had a lot to learn about life and only had to look around to see how fortunate I had been; how fortunate I was...

CHAPTER TWELVE

No Pain, No Gain!

A sling was placed underneath me after I had been dressed in preparation for my first day up in the wheelchair. I didn't mind being hoisted up into mid-air and swung round to hover precariously over the wheelchair while three nurses made sure the positioning was just right. Not at first anyway, but after a few days I began to loathe it. Maybe it was because I knew what I had to go through for the next few hours. The first day was a doddle and when I was told, "that's enough for today," I asked to stay up just a bit longer. Later I would be seen almost pleading to return to my bed. The stiff polystyrene neck collar was unable to support the heaviness of my head on a very weak neck and this caused severe discomfort.

I was on my own now; no mum to fetch and carry for me at a moment's notice, and this was all part of my rehabilitation. Again I had it easier than most. The Jones, who were regular visitors, often tried to be around at tea time to help me with my food, bringing a tasty prawn or salmon sandwich, and it was through them that I met Sue Roberts. We had met before at Haydock and Pontefract and I was very pleased to have her around now. She had appeared earlier on at my bedside armed with baby in one hand and tweezers in the other: "Do you want your eyebrows plucked, chuck?" "Yes, please," was the reply. Sue came in every lunchtime for an hour, 12pm to 1pm. I was in the chair just in time for lunch but the first priority was my hair! It had become thin and wispy and only Sue could make me look reasonably presentable. That was the first thing; then she would take the lid off my lunch tray exclaiming, "You won't get fat on that." A very sad and wrinkled baked potato sat alone, not very appetising. Fortunately food was the last thing I wanted. The letters and cards of support and good wishes were still arriving in handfuls and a funny rhyming letter from a man signed Bond J. kept us well amused. He and I began to correspond over the next few months.

After a few days I was on my way down to look in the physio gym and occupational therapy room. "You will have to cut down on the visitors now," one of the sisters said. But I pretended not to hear. As soon as I was pushed into OT I was placed at the big table, my arms were fastened in slings, hooked to an overhead metal frame that held them out in front of me and suspended in mid-air. "Try and move them in and out," I was instructed by Jill, the head of the OT department. I had to fight to stop the hot tears that welled up in my eyes from tipping over my lashes and running down my face as I viewed my reflection in the window and sat totally demoralised. I could not admit to weakening, even though I felt like it, and the thought of not being able to wipe my face before anyone noticed made me glare defiantly at my reflection as if it was someone else. My voice broke into my thoughts. "Nurse," a blue uniform appeared almost before I had got the word out, "can you hold my head, please?" The relief was unbelievable as she held me under the chin and took the weight off my head, off an aching neck, and once again I became composed. I had crossed a vital bridge and fought off the self pity. It was easier being on my own, with only myself to face, and I hoped I could be as strong when family and friends were there. I found that I could feel very vulnerable and weak if people fussed over me and maybe even then, without realising, I started to detach myself. My defences against tears only slipped a few times when anger and frustration, which unfortunately were fired up by the two people I loved most, were trapped inside me and had no other way of getting out.

Every few days the doctors did their round of the ward, checking the progress and the problems. I tired very quickly, the sister told Dr El Masry, and was continually asking for my head to be held. He suggested a smaller collar but said that it would obviously take time for my neck muscles to strengthen up. The sooner I started exercising with weights in physio the better.

I was taken on in physio by a girl called Mary. She said we would have to work hard on my neck muscles and arms, and after a couple of weeks there were slight signs of improvement. But the odd and horrible feelings that I experienced seemed to heighten as my body was lifted, rolled, pushed and pulled. It lay there motionless whilst all sorts of weird sensations were racing round, screaming at me too move. Sometimes I felt like I was lying on ice, my underside freezing cold, but I was warm as toast to touch.

Mary wasn't too keen at first when I told her she would have to make her television debut. A morning programme called "People Today", hosted by Miriam Stoppard, wanted to do a feature on me. The filming people arrived one morning and the place was in chaos. They were putting "blondes" (their name for bright lights) on high stands, asking the nurses to try and be quiet while they went about their duties, and generally being a bit of a nuisance but the other patients thought it was quite a giggle.

They filmed me most of the morning in the ward, physio and occupational therapy, then in the afternoon we drove to the Jones' racing stables a couple of miles away to get a shot of me near the horses. But by then I was too tired and was having trouble holding my head up, so I stayed in the car trying to look at them out of the passenger window. I'd been there once before to see the horses and it was good to see them, smell them.

It was back to normal the next day for myself and Mary. She would start by gently stretching my neck and, once again, when she held the weight of my head, I could relax my shoulders and the aching would go away for a while. I was soon left by myself lying down on an exercise bed with my head supported in a sling. At each side I had half pound springs attached to a pulley and I had to press my head against the springs until it touched the bed. "Try and do five," Mary said, "then have a rest." The hard work had started but I was used to that, used to pushing myself. The long road to recovery would be littered with disappointment and scattered with the joy of achievement. Even though my life would never be the same, it was important for me to get back to looking and being the person I knew I was. And if I thought I would be able to do something and they told me, "You won't be able to do that," then it made me more determined.

It was unfortunate that Mary left to go abroad at the end of October as we were getting on really well. I was also going in the swimming pool twice a week and felt that I would miss her but another vital lesson was learnt. I could not allow myself to become dependant on one person; there would be other Marys out there but no one is going to be around forever and, as Alan Bailey used to say, "No one is indispensable." I had to be in charge of my own life and I soon realised I could not cling to people.

It is easy and normal for most people in my predicament to rely on someone and I could have done so when I became friendly with Darren, one of the student physiotherapists. While I was waiting to be put back in my chair after doing my exercises, I had noticed the two new male physios and was glad that Sally had supervised me. "I don't want anyone practising on me," I told her brassily. The next day while I lay on the exercise bed, thinking of at least a million places where I'd rather be, a voice asked, "Would you like a mint?"

"No thank you, my mum told me not to take sweeties off strange men," I answered.

He grinned, "Helps with the coffee breath."

"I better have two then, Daza!" We became friends, much to the concern of Sister Garbett. She was very worried about me, after all I was in a very vulnerable state. "She's worried I'm going to fall in love with you and then you're going to run off with a fat nurse!" I said musingly.

Sue pushed me into the physio room and we were surprised that Darren and Keith were already there. "That's handy, Shazza, two physios all to yourself, one for each shoulder." They jumped up to massage my shoulders and we all had a good giggle. It was nice having their attention and, even though I felt fat and unattractive, they didn't seem to notice. They helped and encouraged me with my exercises over the next few months and volunteered to push my bed down to the function room one night where the hospital staff were performing in a pantomime. Everything seemed so matter of fact to them whilst I often cringed with embarrassment because of my situation.

Darren asked me if I was going to the disco on Friday in the function room. "Why, do you want to dance with me?" I said sarcastically. I was thinking that no one would want to be seen socialising with me because I was in a wheelchair and, of course, the emphasis was on dance. "If you like," he said casually, not paying any attention to my curt remark.

It was six weeks since my first day in the chair and I was still having my head held at regular intervals. A follow-up x-ray was taken as progress seemed to be slow. Unfortunately, Dr El Masry said the neck was not mending properly. The reason was because I was unable to hold my head up and it was in flexion too much. He was worried that, as time went by, the neck would set too much in flexion, resulting in my chin being permanently on my chest. I could be fitted with a neck brace which came in three parts and would hold my neck rigid. During the day, therefore my neck would be unable to go into flexion, thus hopefully it would mend satisfactorily. Also, by night in bed, I would have to start sleeping in a different position – almost quite the same as before, only with my neck most definitely in extension. This would be achieved by placing two pillows under my shoulders and letting my head hang back. "I'll do anything," I said. There was no way I was going to end up with my chin on my chest!

Dr El Masry was there to supervise my position when the nurses put me to bed that evening. He said it would be very uncomfortable at first but "should ease a little in time", one of his favourite sayings. It never did. Those nights were most definitely the worst of my life...

Everyone was talking about the disco and I was looking forward to it. It was open to visitors, so Sue, Vicky, another girl Jan (who had been coming in to see me) and my mum were going too. I was in physio when one of the collar specialists brought in the brace. The front and back pieces were mounted on two metal prongs that slotted into a metal plate which was fitted to the body brace. This consisted of firm plastic-covered shoulder grips which were put on first and fastened around the body with soft straps that had adjustable non-slip buckles. "I won't be able to go to the disco in that," I whinged. But it was placed discreetly underneath a high-necked blouse and only the chin cup could be seen. Darren and Keith joined our table and we had a really good time. It didn't bother me watching them dance but I was conscious about my appearance even in the dimly lit room.

The brace was fine for the first few days but it became uncomfortable, digging into my shoulders and the base of my head. It was around this time I started to have cold sweats day and night. I looked terrible, my skin was grey and I had to keep asking people to wipe my face but it was all part of the course and out of my control. I wondered if I'd ever feel normal again. Sometimes I felt as if I was the only one who was not making progress. This injury that is so cruel is lasting for some but not for others. The paralysis can be temporary while nerves are squashed by swelling and bleeding but if they have not been severed, in time, the body is able to regain mobility. Steve, who had had a car crash, and Paul, a rugby accident, had both broken their necks.

So far their injuries had been nursed in the same way as mine but now, as I laid on the exercise plinth, I could only watch as they began to take their first steps back to normality.

I had been adamant from the start that I would return to Newmarket. I had made my home there and would never go back to my Yorkshire roots. TC had been a regular visitor over the last three months and it had been nearly a year since he had left Newmarket. He had made a new life for himself. It gave me great hope and will to know that I could go home to Becklyn. In time I also would have a satisfying life. Perhaps...

I had every right to feel quite excited and a shade apprehensive when I woke up on November 6th. Today I was making the long journey home just for a day visit, via Sheikh Mohammed's helicopter. I had to lie flat for the journey so there would not be too much pressure or strain. We landed in the paddock at the back of the bungalow and it was a peaceful feeling, knowing I was home, even though I couldn't see anything for the moment. The cold air hit my face as the door was opened but it smelt clean and fresh; I didn't recoil at its harshness, I welcomed it. I kept my emotion hidden inside me (like I was getting used to doing) as I looked at the place where I'd had the happiest time of my life and also the saddest. I had left in such a hurry three months before, not giving it a second thought and even though it looked cold and bleak it was the only thing I could salvage from my misfortunes of the past year. I wanted to and needed to.

It was like part of my life was beginning to return as I had some lunch in the Bell Inn with Joss, Jennie and Alison. It didn't matter to us that they had to help me with my food and drink. I was Sharron; they would treat me no differently, no kid gloves, and we joked, "it's the arms and legs that don't work, not the brain." This was much to the distaste of other people, as if I was being reminded cruelly of my loss, but of course I was fully aware.

It was unlikely that I would leave hospital before Christmas but there were a lot of things to organise. I wanted to live as independently as I could and this could only be achieved by employing people to do the everyday things I was unable to do. At the time this was just about everything! A meeting was held to bring together district nurse, social worker and social services. They had to be primed of my needs by the hospital co-ordinators. "You have a voice and a good mind," Dr El Masry had told me, "and you can direct people yourself." It was up to me to say what I wanted or didn't want and it started now. I was used to being in charge and had often been left to hold the fort at Alan Bailey's. And I only wanted to be in charge of my own life! But now, the strength that was admired by some, would be despised by others. They wanted me to fall into line, and this undermined what I wanted.

My brother Clive sat next to me at the meeting and it was a weird feeling to see my mum and dad with lots of strangers all piling into my lounge. The light grey carpet was rubbed and crushed under many shoe-clad feet. The light grey carpet, that had looked so nice even though it was not practical, had taken a hammering. The promise, once made, of it only ever being touched by bare feet was a very distant one. Even my cat, Mr T, knew his place and used to sit in the doorway, paws not exceeding the metal strip that divided the lounge and dining room. That was before a vehicle decided to put him in cat heaven. My neighbour, Jack, dug a hole and I buried Mr T in the garden. I didn't want a replacement, some things can never be replaced... But it seemed an age since then and the best of well laid plans had been ravaged with lodgers and time.

All the people introduced themselves and who they represented. It was agreed that I would need twenty-four hour care for the foreseeable future. "She will need washing and feeding," one of them said, and my happiness at being back where I belonged changed; I felt like an unwanted dog in my own home.

There was a lot to discuss and I would need my own team of lady helpers as well as the input from the district nurse and social services. Here lay another problem, my district nurse was called Peter! "No disrespect, Peter, but you won't be coming in to see me," I said, and the eyebrows on faces around me raised. There was no way a male nurse was going to wash me or put me on the loo... I had "problem" written all over me to those in authority but to me it read, "This is my life". My social worker tried to reason with me, "If he is your district nurse you'll have to have him."

"I won't and I'm not." There were two female district nurses who worked a different patch. If I could not be accommodated it would be a poor show. I could hear them all whispering and see them nodding as they packed up their papers to go. I knew they were going to try and persuade me, they were 50's and drifting! I suppose my dad was quite surprised at my stance but I'd grown up having to make my own decisions. I was his daughter but he didn't really know me. He knew one thing: I said what I thought and some of those words had hurt his feelings; but sometimes things hurt, and that's life.

Becklyn seemed a lifetime away that evening as I was tucked up in my hospital bed. I felt tired but was fairly satisfied with the day's events. I had a goal now, a target, to return home and carry on with my life the best I could. In the meantime there was plenty to be getting on with although I became very disheartened at the slow progress and seemingly endless pain. The physios tried all sorts of different pain relieving machines but nothing worked. My right shoulder blade, arm and all muscle in and around them were affected by the paralysis. It was a vicious circle as limited or near non-existing movement of my neck put strain on my shoulder, and vice versa.

My request for a day out to the races was met with a little surprise from Dr El Masry but he agreed, although why I wanted to return to Bangor-on-

Dee racecourse, on a freezing cold day at the end of November was a mystery to him. I suppose the strong feeling I had to get back to my life made me want to go. I was fed up with being hospitalised, fed up with the routine, fed up with the medical words, fed up with seeing urine bags hanging on the side of the beds, and sick and fed up with the smell. It didn't upset me to see the racecourse, the last place where I'd walked. I looked across to the last hurdle and thought of how many hooves had thundered over the spot (including TC on his first winner of the season) where I had lain, unaware of the life that was ahead, unaware that I would never walk or ride a horse again. Elain Mellor's voice said, "Hello," and the small hospitality box was filled to capacity with jockeys, trainers and valets coming to wish me well. I wasn't emotional, much to the surprise of some. This was where I belonged, in this fresh tough world, no room for wimps. It was a world of brave horses and jockeys, it was hectic, it was racing, it was something I loved. I had a wonderful day.

My outings to the Jones' yard or to Sue's house were terrific for my rehabilitation. Most Saturdays Sue and her husband, Steve, would take me to their house for sausage in a crusty white roll, hot coffee out of a proper cup (there were only plastic ones in hospital) and I could watch the racing on telly in front of a roaring coal fire. Holly and Alice, Sue's daughters of six and seven, did their fair share to see that I was comfortable. What more could one ask for?

It was around this time that, through the unfortunate accident of a local lad called Alan, I met the Oswestry Rugby Club boys. Alan had broken his neck playing rugby at Birmingham. When he eventually was allowed visitors, it was often six burly lads with voices to match. They were soon coming over into my side ward which I shared with seventeen-year-old Samantha, who I nicknamed the monster and she in turn called me the horror. She had been thrown out of the back window in a car crash. She sustained a broken neck and would never walk again. We used to try and push our chairs round the wards but more often than not she would end up behind me, to give me a push. We were in a bit of trouble because we refused to eat in the dining room, preferring to stay in our side ward. We were alright and were coping in our own way, and it was at a time when a lot of the male patients were very bitter and angry. We didn't want to put up with the abusive language or food throwing that took place and resembled a chimps' tea party. It was good for our rehabilitation, the nurses said. "What, the bad language?" Sam inquired. "Or a crusty roll round the back of the head?" I piped up. We refused to eat at meal times and they soon turned a blind eye because they knew we were right. I think we helped each other along, even when we were sitting up in bed opposite each other, in silence and unable to talk; our bad days.

Diana Jones often trained with the rugby lads and she introduced them to me. She also went out with one called Peter who had earned the name "Dangerous" when he was on the pitch. They would often pop in to see us and said they would take me to the Christmas party at the Rugby Club if I would like to go. We had a really good night out and they put on a sort of pantomime; seeing all of those big lads in fancy dress was quite a show stopper! I gave Big Frank eleven out of ten for his singing – he was extremely good. So now I had lots of new friends – Robin (who is older than he thinks he is), Glynn (the farmer), Frank, who wasn't called Frank at all but was nicknamed after "ole blue eyes" himself for his rendition of "My Way", Sean, who would often push me down to the Snack Shack for a coffee after lunch, Platty, Brett and Trevor who were often popping in but would rather me pop out to the pub, the Last Inn, on a Sunday dinner time. I would often return on a Sunday afternoon tired, cold and with mud on my shoes – my only explanation, "I've been with the rugby boys – all of them!"

Visiting finished at 8pm and, by the time everybody had said their goodnights and were settled down with the lights dimmed, it was usually about half an hour later. The last hot drink of the day was served at 9pm. The nurse started at the entrance of the ward and made her way down towards Karen, Samantha and myself who occupied the last three beds. It was turned 8.30pm when the doors of the television room that linked the Wrekin Ward with the more rehabilitated Gladstone Ward opened quietly. I didn't take any notice until I heard, "Shaz are you awake?" It was Robin and Glynn, two of the rugby boys back from a skiing holiday. I told them that visiting was over but they sneaked in and sat on the floor by my bed, popping up every now and again to show me photos of their holiday. The giggles were becoming louder as the nurse set off with her tea trolley and I was telling them they must go but they were still there as the nurse reached Karen, who by now also had the giggles. She asked the nurse for something that sent her back up the ward and Robin and Glynn fled unnoticed. When she came back she asked what the joke was as we three were now in fits of laughter. She then accused Karen of having a crafty cigarette which was forbidden in the ward; even more than late callers!

Sometimes I'd wake up and one of the lads would be sitting there. "Just called in after work," they would say. I would be embarrassed, wondering if I'd been asleep with my mouth open, but they were very tactful, they never said if I had been. This was in marked contrast to Darren (I'm too sexy for this chair) who constantly reminded me that I looked like s.h. one t.! – in the nicest possible way of course. I rated Darren, though. He was always so positive and, when he was asked if he had had a good Christmas at home, he said with a smile on his face that it had been wonderful, and he meant it. Darren had recently been demobbed from the army, so with a few friends he had decided to take a holiday in Spain. After an early morning swim in the sea they returned to the hotel and Darren went to look at how inviting the hotel pool was. Unfortunately, as he approached the edge he slipped, falling head first into the waterless pit. He broke his neck, the damage was irreversible. I felt guilty because I did not enjoy Christmas at all.

I returned to the ward after a particularly satisfying swimming session, only to be told off yet again. The Sister on duty scolded me before my bed had even got back into place. The routine of being made ready for a swimming session consisted of swimsuit on after being washed in the morning, then a porter would push the bed outside across to the swimming pool. Bearing in mind that it was winter and bloody freezing cold, more towels and blankets were put on the bed. Ron, one of the porters, always used to wrap a towel around my head to keep me warm for the short outward journey but when the doors opened the cold air was still harsh. On the way back it was even more important to be kept warm and we were wrapped up in towels, virtually mummified, and only a small face could be seen. We would have to stay like that for an hour or so to make sure body temperature did not drop. So here I lay, unable to move anything but my mouth, which was by now wide open in exasperation. "I've told you about visitors coming too early, visiting starts at 12.00pm not 11.00am."

"I don't suppose you found out who it was?" I asked.

She replied gruffly, "Somebody called John Francome [Seven times Champion Jump Jockey and now racing TV commentator] or something like that, I've sent him down to the Snack Shack." The Snack Shack was in need of a good make-over and I hoped he didn't drink the tea!

I had never been introduced to John before and what a way to meet somebody – just a face in a towel. And I don't think for one minute he believed all the things I was telling him I could do... In fact afterwards he told me he thought I would be forever hospitalised. Another visit from him just before Christmas found me quite subdued. He had brought smoked salmon, a loaf of brown bread, champagne and a few copies of his book, *How to Win Betting*, which he signed and gave to some of the other lads in the OT department as he chatted to them as well. Even the Sister knew who he was by then!

My unexpected visit from Lester Piggott caused quite a stir too. A recently injured man in another side ward lay facing the door one quiet Sunday lunchtime. The next minute, after seeing a man in a raincoat glance at him as he passed, he shouted, "Nurse, nurse!" When she came he said, "I think I've just seen Lester Piggott," and she said,

"Yeah, and I'm Florence Nightingale." After a while word got round that it really was Lester Piggott and all of a sudden my nursing care was stepped up as excuses were made to see my well known visitor.

Most of the boys at the same stage as me, post injury, were allowed home for Christmas, as was Samantha. The ward had been decorated and the nurses fixed tinsel in their hair. They kept saying "Merry Christmas" but I couldn't feel excited. "What's merry about it?" came the reply. I just kept wishing it was over. Christmas morning found me very gloomy. Last year, I was riding *Howjal* in preparation for our race on Boxing Day at Huntingdon. Last year, I spent the rest of the day alone. To be in the same position now would be welcomed. No amount of cards or presents could compensate for how I felt and it was hard not to seem ungrateful. I was still deeply shocked at the news of Marilyn Bailey's death in a car crash, just weeks before, and felt so helpless. I didn't want Alan and Jan to have to experience all that pain of tragedy. I had watched her grow up for the past ten years and it was so unjust. Everything had once been so rosy and, in a few short months, our lives had been devastated by fate. And if that wasn't enough, the fatal racing fall of jockey Philip Barnard on Boxing Day at Wincanton made us gasp for breath in disbelief.

My mum, Justine, brother Mark and Helen his wife arrived. We were going to the Wynnstay Hotel for Xmas lunch. I'd managed to secure the OT flat, so at least I didn't have to go back on the ward for the next few days. The flat is adjacent to the hospital. It comprises of kitchen, sitting room, bathroom and two small bedrooms, just far enough away for privacy, near enough for attention. It serves a good purpose; giving families and couples the chance to be alone and cope with their new situation. I lightened up a little while the nurses washed and dressed me. They didn't deserve to have their day totally ruined by my feistiness and by the time my relatives arrived I had adjusted my attitude. My mum had brought enough food to feed an army for our stay in the flat; it was just as well, for friends came and went frequently for the next few days.

Christmas and New Year passed, so now with festivities over it was back to serious work. One day I'd feel as if I was improving and another I took two steps back. Jenny, one of the senior physios, had said she would like me to go on the tilt table. This is an electrical plinth with a base at one end for your feet to stand on. The purpose is to get your body in an upright position, thus enabling all internal organs to function in their normal position. I hated it. Strapped on at the chest, waist and knees, I felt like the bride of Frankenstein as I slowly began to rise. All these things seemed so abnormal to me and I wanted to be so normal. I was never pushed into going on it again and steered clear for a few weeks.

The week after New Year found me still bleak and a little awkward. I kept thinking of all the things I couldn't do, so when Sally asked me what I'd like to do in physio one Monday I said I'd like to go in the standing frame. The wooden frames have thick sheepskin-wrapped leather straps; one goes in front of your knees and the other round your bottom, keeping your legs rigid so they don't buckle. Some people with even limited use of their arms and hands can stand without any assistance once they are upright. I had already been told it was doubtful that I'd ever be able to use a standing frame. Not only would two people have to hold my upper body but the pressure would be so great that my body would not be able to cope and I would not remain conscious. "You'll have to go on the tilt table for a few days for your body to get used to being vertical," Sally reasoned. I thought about it. I did want to try and stand up, so for the next few days I was the bride of Frankenstein, only now I was joking about it. I was totally upright by the third day but the blood soon began to drain out of my face. When I started to hear that funny fuzzy sound in my ears, then feel the warm prickly sensation on my head and neck, I knew it was time to go more horizontal. "How long was I at max?" I asked my brother Clive who was timing me in maximum upright position. He told me. "I'll do better tomorrow," I mocked, not letting him see how discouraged I felt at the pathetic twenty seconds…

Friday came; it had been like waiting for a ride and now it was here. My wheelchair was put into place in front of the frame. I had to be lifted out of the chair, over the frame's ledge, while the straps were fastened. "Alright, Sharron, we are going to stand you up now. If you start to feel giddy we'll just lay you forward again." Sally and Jane were really nice but I had been bullish about standing up and for them to see me go green and never mention the standing frame again would have given them a little bit of satisfaction, I think. The corset to help my blood pressure was in place and the next minute there I was, standing up, face to face with the world for the first time in five months! It was really weird – I couldn't feel my legs, I couldn't feel anything, I even wondered if it was happening at all. The fuzzy sound began in my ears but I concentrated hard on just breathing. Sally and Jane were holding me up, bracing themselves with both hands against the unsteady cargo. They kept asking me if I was okay, and I just made an "umm" sound, worried about being distracted from breathing in case I passed out.

I was surprised when the fuzzy sound deep in my ears disappeared. Now I knew I could fight it off by breathing properly. It is easy to hold your breath without realising, and I had done that in my early days of getting up in the chair. "I think that is enough for today," Sally said and, with the fuzziness beginning to return, I agreed. I had been standing for five minutes. It was a big boost for me; a leap forward.

The encouragement from people had in no way subsided. Cards, letters and flowers still adorned my bedside. I had made many new friends and met lots of new people. My enthusiasm to work in physio was boosted by the frequent visits from fellow jockeys such as Gee Armytage, Tanya Sherwood, Celia Radband and Kelly Marks amongst many others. They were not close friends of mine and I didn't expect them to visit me. Jimmy Quinn, who I had worked so hard at Alan Bailey's, turned up one day on his own. This day may not have been one of his best but he had brightened up mine. I was amazed at the thoughtfulness of complete strangers. One man even did a detour from the motorway with his delivery of shoes from the manufacturer's to a shop. His name was Bobby Moore and he hoped I didn't mind him just popping in. I didn't, even if he wasn't a famous footballer. Then there was Mark, who owned a store in Llandudno and brought me lots of goodies, but the nurses were not too happy when I asked if they could toast a currant teacake for me at nine o'clock at night. Unfortunately some others did become a bit of a nuisance and I sometimes pretended to be asleep or was working in physio. Some days, if you felt you just wanted to be left alone, it was hard to cope with strangers. They don't know you, they don't understand you and so they chat persistently, trying to make you feel better. With family and friends, conversation was not always needed and they were just there for me.

Dr El Masry did his usual morning round and, after the morning greetings, I asked him, "It's about time I was going home, don't you think?"

"Yes, I suppose it is," he replied smiling. He usually decided when it was time for a patient to leave, not the other way round. I began to count the days after I was given a leaving date and, all being well, February 14th had been earmarked. The wheels were in motion and I gleefully told everyone. But Karen from Birmingham, who was back in hospital for a while, warned me saying, "You think you want to get home now, but after a few days you'll be wishing you were back." I couldn't even begin to think that that would be right.

So now I even looked forward to my birthday and it proved to be a good day. I still had not been forgotten by my fellow jockeys, male and female, and the cards and flowers proved that. Sean, one of the rugby boys, turned up at lunch time while Sue was opening my cards, which was nice. TC arrived a little later and we all went to the Snack Shack for coffee. I had to go to OT and then into physio. I was pleased TC stayed for the afternoon to witness and help me reach a landmark. I stood for a whole half hour! I had been emotional with him earlier, blubbing on about realising I would never have a normal life again, and that was unfair for him. Unfortunately, my mum, dad and Justine arrived too late to see me standing. It did amuse me though, as we all sat in the Snack Shack for yet another coffee, mum with her ex-husband and me with my ex-fiance; it was like a sitcom! Vicky Jones had arranged for quite a few of us to go out for a meal at the Indian restaurant in the evening and we had a really good night. It nearly ended with me on the ward floor when Micky (Clare), who I met through Vicky, caught his jacket on the arm of the chair as they were lifting me into bed. There was a moment's panic before I reached the bed safely, amidst a lot of giggling and shushing. The day ended with me feeling fairly high on emotion, but not a sad emotion. Perhaps now I had realised I could still enjoy myself, and I felt lucky to have these special people around me.

Wide awake and unable to sleep I asked the nurse for the telephone. "It's quarter to one in the morning, Sharron." I wanted to call my mum and tell her how the night had gone, I told the nurse, and carried on to say she wouldn't mind if I woke her up. She didn't. She answered the reverse charge call and we chatted for ages. Later, when it came to light the call had cost her £54.00, I asked her if she minded. She didn't!

There had never been any discussion about where I would live when I left hospital, it had not been an issue. Newmarket was my home and I wanted to live independently of my family. Before I could manage to set myself up with the round-the-clock care I needed, the hospital co-ordinator said I really had to be back in my own area. That meant I would have to go into a nursing home. There were a few about but the preference was a young disabled unit. Alison Thom made enquiries and the one that seemed most suitable was at Littleport which is about fifteen miles away from Newmarket. I had become restless and seemed to have progressed as much as I could for now, so there was no reason to prolong my stay. I had been incarcerated for long enough and wanted to go back to my life, I wanted to go home...

One of my last nights out in Oswestry was at a benefit do in the Wynnstay hotel, organised mainly by Vicky Jones. It was wonderful. Lots of my Newmarket friends came and met a lot of my Oswestry friends, not to mention the jockeys, trainers and other racing people that attended. Seven days later I flew home, once again in Sheikh Mohammed's helicopter, on February 14th 1992.

GOD...
grant me
the Serenity to accept
the things I cannot change...
Courage to change
the things I can and Wisdom
to know the difference.

(Prayer)

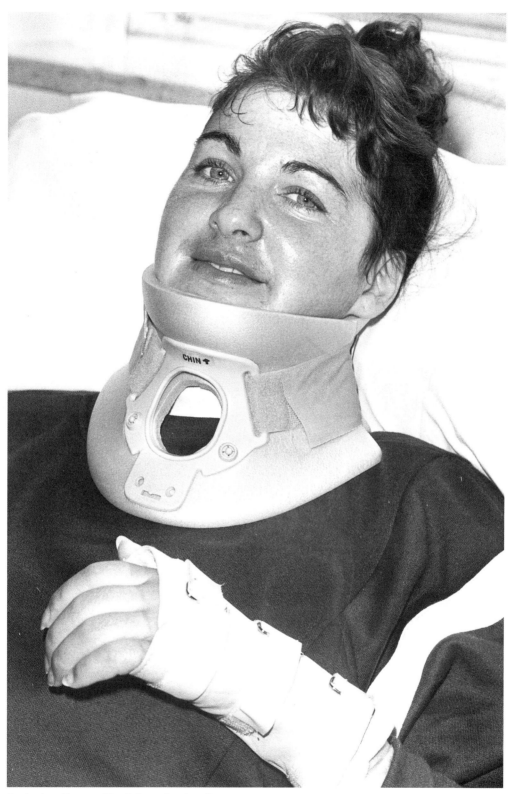

In physio at Oswestry Hospital, wearing the collar.

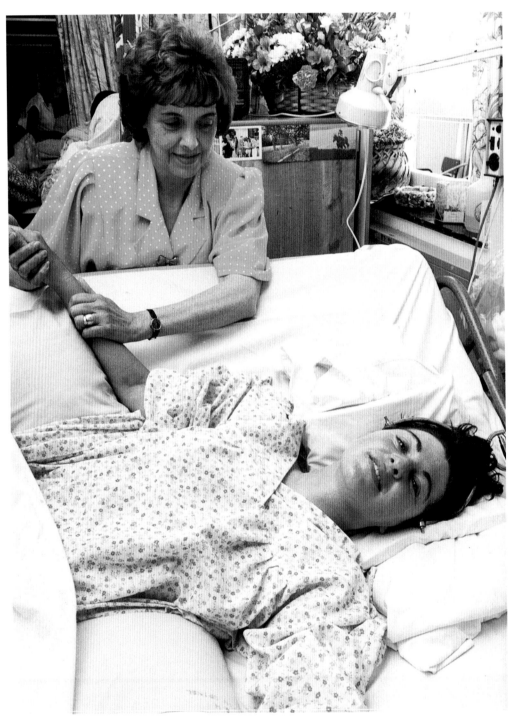

Crucifix position, high tilting bed.

Photograph by Telegraph & Argus.

Lester's Awards, March 1995, London Hilton Hotel with Lord Oaksey.

Photograph by Trevor Jones (Racing Post).

"Day visit to Becklyn" with Jenny Crossley, Joss Drake and Alison Thom, November 1991.

Photograph by Vernon Place
(Newmarket Journal)

Leaving Oswestry. Left to right: Di Jones, Steve Roberts, Alex Jones, Sue Roberts, Vicky and Alison Thom, February 1992.

Injured Jockey's Party in Tenerife, February 1995.

Photograph by Peter Dun.

Fund raising night at the Wynnstay Hotel, February 1992. From left to right: Trevor Wall, Elain Mellor, Bob Davis, Celia Radband, Vicky Jones, Terry Prothero, Lord Oaksey, Jim McGrath, Bill Woodward (owner) and Jo Lodder.

Photograph by Bob Williams.

My Family, from left to right: Alyshia Leonne, Justine (sister), Stacey, Mother, Kelly (Niece),
Clive (Brother), Bonita (sister-in-law), Helen (sister-in-law) holding James (nephew), Mark (brother) with Matthew (nephew).

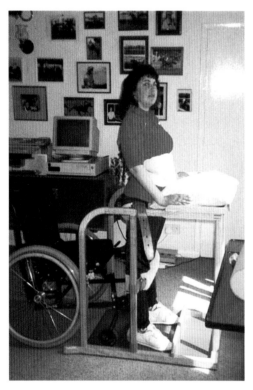

Using the standing frame at home.

Me and my team of ladies at a party. From left to right: Nancy (kneeling), Dawn, Michelle, Janet, Joan and Carey.

Practising my carriage driving skills with co-driver Mrs Shirley Reeder, with "Buccaneer", March 1995.

Photograph by Alan Walter, Sunday Express

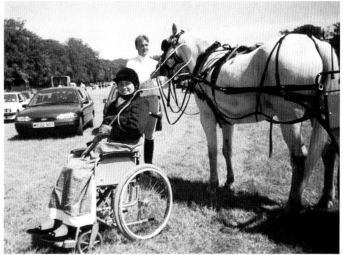

Ready for the off – again!

Back on board with a little help from Andy Young and friends.

Back to Bangor. Left to right: Jo Lodder, John Shortt and Trevor Wall, November 1991.

Photograph by Shropshire Star.

CHAPTER THIRTEEN

Returning to Becklyn

I said my goodbyes to the crowd of people who had gathered to wish me well, then, as the helicopter began to ascend, it swooped round for one last look. The next time I saw them it would be me who was the visitor. Vicky and Alison travelled with me and I wondered if my Newmarket friends would become as proficient at handling me as my Oswestry ones were.

The journey was terrific and, as we approached the bungalow, the helicopter swung round so I had a clear view of the "welcome home" banner that had been placed on the roof. Terry Jennings, Bryn Crossley and Penny (who I used to work with) had precariously tip-toed onto the slanting roof, putting the banner in place. My mum, sister Justine, brother Mark, and quite a few close friends were waiting, along with the press and Anglia Television. The only people missing were the Baileys. Ironically they were moving out of Induna that very same day. They were making a fresh start with a new home and stables in Cheshire. The champagne was opened and I knew it still wouldn't be plain sailing but if I could not make a life for myself here, then it would never happen anywhere else. Even now the house, which had been neglected, held a warmth and compassion. The laughter and tears that were ingrained in each room would forever be a reminder but for now I wanted that. I suppose it's like when someone dies, you don't just forget them. I didn't want to pretend my love and life had never taken place and, as I was caught up in the familiar ambience of my home, I felt safe.

I didn't want to stay out at Littleport but, until proper care had been found, I had no option. I was booked in for eight weeks and hopefully in that time, with help from the right places, I should be able to find myself a workforce.

I tried to keep my spirits high but I had moments of sheer desperation during those first two weeks. This was through no fault of the staff or people who ran the home but because of my own expectations of what life for me now was going to be like. The girls were good at their job but they were not trained to deal with the trauma or rehabilitation which I didn't realise I was going through. So they giggled about the evening before and which lad they fancied whilst I sat naked on a plastic chair waiting to be hoisted up and over into the bath. My body, once fit and strong, had now let go. Leg and stomach muscles, finally surrendering to the immobility, made me feel fat and ugly but the helpers, young and lively, were oblivious to my feelings… to my pride and dignity.

Alison was marvellous; she picked me up every day, bar one or two when Wendy Jennings came and took me out. Alison came about one o'clock and sometimes we'd go to Becklyn or to her house, stopping off to see Joss at work, then I would stay in the car whilst Alison did a few jobs at the stables. By the time she took me back I was exhausted and would go straight to my room. I had a fear of being just left in the sitting room with the other residents and I had this wicked impression of everybody sitting and just staring out of the window. This, surely was not the way for me to spend the rest of my life. My family and friends all rallied round with a bit of help from me. Joss put the adverts in the paper, Alison and David asked around for people who could help. I needed a certain amount of medical attention, so that had to be arranged. The house had to be cleaned and decorated, so my mum along with Uncle Michael and their friend Maureen Dunn set to that task. Operation "Home" began...

Two weeks later, under the supervision of David and Alison, a gathering of would-be helpers assembled at Becklyn. If the friend of Janet Boston's daughter, who'd had nursing training, could start in the morning, I was "evens" to stay at home. Petra was pretty and blonde, and for now quiet and shy, mainly due to the fact that she was foreign. After what seemed a very brief interview she was happy to start in the morning. I felt quite light; no more Littleport. I could now leave before the eight weeks were up. Another girl offering her services was also a pretty blonde called Emma. She was introduced to me by Maureen Barnard. Unfortunately, the work did not suit her and she left within a week. But I had been warned by the co-ordinator that a turnover in staff was to be expected. Even though Petra was doing 8am till 4pm Monday to Friday there were still lots of hours to fill. It was a nightmare doing rotas and continued to be one for some time. Janet, who still worked at David Thom's, did a few nights and so that helped. Maureen Barnard temporarily cooked for me and there were other people who volunteered to work until I could get some permanent staff, so I could stay at home.

It was with mixed feelings I woke up in my bedroom after so long. Maybe deep inside I thought everything would return to normal when I came home but, of course, I was no way near conquering the situation that had been bestowed on me. The hospital-type single bed with an inflatable mattress, which was designed to tilt left, right, up and down, manually or on timer had woken me up several times during the night. Even though the hum was low and the movement slow and everybody else thought it was wonderful, I wished I could lie back in my own bed, but it wasn't practical as it was too low. It was essential for me to have two-hourly turns that, hopefully, would keep me free of bedsores, and the girls also needed a higher bed so they would not hurt their backs bending over to wash and dress me. I had a lot to learn; I had crossed over into a different world where every one of my actions had to involve another person. The only thing I could do for myself was think. Dr El Masry had told me to make the decisions, to take control; now I had to stay in control!

Petra arrived on Monday morning, shortly followed by Anne, the district nurse (one – nil to me, not that I was counting!) Then Petra didn't feel well. "She won't last long," I scoffed to the nurse but perhaps it was an attack of nerves more than anything else. Petra proved to be a piece of gold. It wasn't easy for her but she coped admirably. There were often awkward situations and my mood could change quickly but she soon sensed when I needed to be alone. The silences could be long but we were never ill at ease. We established a routine during the day and, after I'd been washed and dressed, I'd sit up in bed reading the papers. At first we put a paper clip at the top and bottom of the page to stop them sliding all over the place but they were soon replaced by staples. They were then propped up against a pillow on a piece of thin non-stick rubber stuff that I brought home from the hospital. A hands-free phone sat on my left side and some days I'd stay there till early afternoon as I still tired quickly in the wheelchair. Petra got on with washing, ironing and making tea and coffee, my bedroom often busier than Piccadilly Circus with people popping in. It was good for me and I thrived on entertaining as I had in hospital.

I didn't make any immediate plans. I felt tired and emotionally drained. There were still lots of TC's belongings to sort out and, although I liked to hear from him, and see him, it became increasingly difficult for me to handle. I took each day as it came. I was having physio twice a week with Gabrielle (the physio from hell!) and arrangements were being made to visit the out-patients department at Newmarket hospital. I had met Gabrielle, a New Zealander, whilst staying at Littleport and we got on well from day one. A standing frame had been ordered and the sooner I could get upright again the better. There was a lot of work to go though and we'd already devised a good way of trying to get some more movement into my neck. I could not turn my head left or right but, with the help of a shiny calendar adorned by Adonis (the American male dance/strip group) placed underneath, I began to slowly slide it from side to side. It became an important part of my physio.

Everything was in a right muddle but did it really matter? It did not... I was home. A few changes needed to be made so things would be more accessible, and it was a tight squeeze in the dining room with the plinth, standing frame and computer, the latter perched on the sideboard with its matching table and chairs now safely back with their previous owner (Aunty Linda). The hoist that had been put in the narrow blue bathroom was complete with plastic chair. There was only just enough room to swing round. Petra had to wind it up a bit before unclipping the wheels and then climb over the bath from behind me to in front. "Good job you're not a fat nurse," I told her.

Anne Carr, the district nurse, helped Petra three days a week with the bath but I still needed another person. She would eventually withdraw her services as I became accustomed to being at home. Wendy Jennings knew of a girl and, like Petra, she had done some nursing training. Becky joined us and also came to live at Becklyn. Things were coming together gradually and the two younger girls coped well with their new job. It was hard for us all to begin with. Working and living in such close proximity with people who you have nothing in common with is very difficult but we all got on quite well.

Jennie called in most days. She corresponded with the Independent Living Fund so I could pay my staff. I was grateful she did a better job than the people who were supposed to help! She also assisted Terry and Wendy Jennings with a fund-raising night at the Cabaret Club. I was lucky, so damned lucky, to have all these people around me. I owed them. She kept me well informed as to what was going on and it was planned to coincide with Newmarket's Craven meeting in April.

Going out didn't worry me. I'd already dressed up for Oswestry and the Jockeys' awards and, even though I would always find lots of faults with my new body image, I didn't want to be ungrateful by turning my nose up at my appearance when the girls had tried so hard to please me. A lot of my clothes were no longer suitable (the little black number was now redundant). I bought a few glitzy tops and mixed old with new. I kept telling myself to get on with it; there was no turning the clock back!

There was definitely a change of friendliness from both men and women who knew me. It seemed the most distant of acquaintances were welcoming me as a long lost bosom buddy, whilst some male friends, from whom I felt a hug and kiss would be in order, were avoiding any eye contact and just smiling with a whispered hello before turning to talk to someone else. There was no getting away from it; I would be treated differently by some, maybe because the odd hug or kiss would be misinterpreted by me. I knew it was hard for them and I understood. I just hoped in time they would see me as the same person with the same feelings...

Who Will Love Me Now, Mum...

OoO

Heart beats gently striving to be free...
In the quiet of my room... In my darkened solitude
I ask you... As I try to move a limb
Who will love me now, mum
Now my body lies motionless to everything

Music plays loudly begging me to dance...
And the sun shines gently... Hoping I can
Down on my face I turn to close
My eyes...
Who will love me now, mum
So sad... Your daughter cries...

Home that warms me keeping me strong...
Now filled with strangers
Who do not belong...
So who will love me now, mum
I cannot get up and go
For a run in the park... Or a quiet stroll

And my treasures lay waiting...
Just longing to be held
In anticipation
Waiting for me to mend...
But who will love me now, mum...
Who will be my friend...

OoO

Sharron Murgatroyd

CHAPTER FOURTEEN

Life Sitting Down

I was reluctant to make permanent changes to the bungalow and, when suggestions were made, I just said, "yeah", not even looking up from my paper. I was in no hurry to do anything. There was a lot going on around me to fill the days and I remained caught up in the novelty of what had happened. Representatives of the press and TV still asked me to re-live that fateful day, which felt like only yesterday. My spiel was now so well rehearsed that I hardly had to think about it. "Every jump jockey knows the risks involved. I'm not saying I wouldn't like to turn the clock back, but it has happened and I have to make the most of it." I believed in what I said and I suppose the romance of calling myself a jump jockey and doing something I loved to do clouded the severity of how I had been left. "A high price to pay," they would argue and I wonder if, sub-consciously, I had not admitted to myself that I would indeed spend the rest of my days sitting down, while seemingly appearing very well adjusted. I became tired just by talking, my mouth trying to compensate for the loss of limbs! So with that, physio, days of an aching, burning body and sleepless nights, I had to pace myself. My one promise was that I would never stay in bed all day no matter how awful I felt, even if I was only up for a couple of hours. I was plagued with bladder infections but had been fore-warned that this would happen and they dictated my mood and strength.

I missed my old life desperately. I missed the smell and feel of the horses. I had loved horses for a very long time, as long as I could remember. I missed the freedom and the closeness. The relationship with horses can be so special, they know when you are happy and they certainly know when you are sad. Even so, I was in no hurry to go and sit round at the stables. I had been an all or nothing person and my friend Joss used to scold me sometimes for being so blatant. At other times, though, she would thank me for my black and white attitude which put things into perspective instead of delving for problems that did not exist. David and Alison Thom, Sean Woods, Jeff and Lydia Pearce often asked me to visit their stables but I only went a couple of times. What I didn't face up to could not hurt me. I thought it would have been alright if Alan and Jan Bailey were still at Induna but, of course, that was just another excuse. Lucy Hide, who is Sean's girlfriend and also rode as a lady jockey, picked me up one day in her yellow MG convertible and, after a cruise around Newmarket with the wind in our hair, we went back to the stables. I enjoyed it but felt this annoying frustration. One day I would have horses in my life again but for now I had to get used to my new way of living. I started to push away the things I could not do. What was the point of watching the horses exercising? It might make me feel useless and I wasn't useless... was I?

I needed to take a back seat for a while. The last eight months had taken their toll and before that I had been so determined to ride well and do things right, so determined to win and prove myself. Now I'd had enough of fighting the good fight. I did what I had to do, nothing more, nothing less. I concentrated on getting stronger and only did what suited me. This way I felt in command. To raise my right arm another inch by the end of the week would seem a reasonable goal but I didn't set myself any sort of task. The disappointment would far outweigh the achievement. If movement was to return, I felt it would come with time and strength. I didn't see any reason to get frustrated and worked up over something that was impossible for me at the moment. My sense of humour made light of my awkwardness but I was aware that I couldn't have it all my own way. Nevertheless I kept alert. I'd always had a mind of my own, it would not change now; no one was going to get one over on me and probably, without realising it, by not wasting vital energy pushing my body into doing something it was not capable of, I kept mentally strong.

I read the racing paper religiously and kept a keen interest in what was going on. This was therapy in itself. The left arm was often tired and struggling before I'd reached the greyhound section! The right was unable to offer any help at all.

I loved to see my friends ride winners and when a ladies' race at Lingfield was run in May, I urged Jennie to take a ride. I was thrilled to present the prizes for the Sharron Murgatroyd and Centre Parcs Race. It was a good turn out and I was pleased the Princess Royal also agreed to ride. She was the main attraction for the public and media. The proceeds went to the Injured Jockeys' Fund. The result was great, with *Ballerina Bay* ridden by Di Jones and trained by the Thoms winning, and Jennie finishing second.

By the summer Social Services introduced me to three new women who would do two hours per evening. They would take it in turns a few days at a time to come and cook me a meal. That was six girls now. Petra and Becky did the main times, Janet the odd nights and now Nancy and Carey, who both lived in the village, and Sharon who lived at Mildenhall. It was funny seeing all these different women in my house, in my cupboards, touching my possessions. A different nurse came in at weekends and I held the reins but didn't always feel like steering. I just wanted them to get on with whatever they had to and, before everything was running smoothly, a year had gone by.

It had taken a while to sort out but at last I had my "Possum" fixed up. Possum means "Am Able" in Latin. It is a vital piece of equipment for people in my position. With the lightest touch on an infra-red box the size of a pocket calculator, it brings up a menu on the combined computer screen. This was set up so I could use the television, video and telephone in the lounge and television in the bedroom. It was brilliant to actually be in control of something. As the relevant item is highlighted on the screen, you touch the box and it shows all the functions of a remote control. No more calling for assistance with that! I could flick over to my hearts content. I soon had the telephone directory full and it certainly was an asset.

By late summer my week started with a visit to the osteopath, Stephen Gold. He tried to relieve the tightness of muscles around my shoulders and neck. "Some days are worse than others," I told him. There was no pattern to the pain and burning sensation. If I rested it could be just as bad as when I was tired. "Can you think of any times when you don't have pain?" he asked, trying to make sense of it all.

"Oh, yes, when I've had a few glasses of red wine." He told me that did make sense. When the alcohol gets into the bloodstream, it stimulates the circulation within the muscles, so they relax instead of being taut. "It knocks off a few neurones as well." He explained that the small cells that make up the brain slowly have their lights put out, which is why in my case the pain eases and, depending on how much is taken, the words slur, other people stagger, eventually falling over drunk. I smiled, "But I can't go round permanently p..... can I?"

I had physio at 9.30am at home on a Tuesday, went swimming Wednesday afternoons, attended physio at Newmarket out-patients on Thursday mornings where, for a short period of time, I also tried acupuncture (did I really need to put myself through all this pain?). Another tried and failed remedy. Then physio again on Fridays at 1.30pm. The days of staying in bed until early afternoon were over. Saturday I laid in till 10am and was washed, dressed and up in the chair ready to watch the Chart Show at 11.30am whilst reading my paper. Then BBC racing followed by Channel Four Racing followed by Brookside. I was usually guaranteed Sunday lunch out with Jennie and Bryn or just with the girls (if my mum and family were not staying) where, by the evening, all pain and many more neurones were gone, replaced by fits of laughter and lots of fun, for a short while anyway. There were good times to reminisce and we did, wishing the Tardis would appear and take us all back in time (but not as far as the Jurassic age). "Shazzy would still ride four lots out for David Thom!" someone said...

I had made few appearances in the town but only because it didn't really interest me. I was never one for just window shopping. I did find it frustrating, though, if I saw someone I knew and they would be too embarrassed to stop and speak to me. I wanted them to see I was still a person whom they could speak to and did they really think I hadn't seen them before they crossed over the road? My other senses began to compensate. I was noticing more things, hearing more distinctive sounds and sometimes I felt quite disguised as I was pushed through the crowd with only the odd smile of recognition. The never ending "excuse me please," said in a very loud voice by my pusher who was becoming irate at people who did not look where they were going, made me feel a nuisance and in the way. But I kept telling my pushers to be polite, people were not always expecting a wheelchair under their feet.

There was a definite nip to the air but I still insisted on going out for an hour or so, around 4pm. I had a new friend and I looked forward to spending a little time with him. He kissed my face in his own way and nuzzled at my hair gently. He always seemed pleased to see me and didn't even notice the wheelchair. His name was *Fiefdom* and he was a horse. He had won his last race the previous February at the age of twelve and I told Wilf Storey, his trainer, I could give him a home on retirement. *Fiefdom* had started his racing life in Newmarket with Bruce Hobbs and had since travelled many miles. He had provided a lot of people with precious memories and it was right and fitting that he should spend the rest of his days being appreciated. Maureen and John kept their horse, *Della*, at Becklyn and they were more than pleased to look after him for me. It was good to see the two nearly identical chestnuts grazing happily in the paddock.

I had also acquired another of God's creatures in need of a home, thanks mainly to a friend Jill who gave the beautifully marked, over friendly feline a drop of milk. I didn't want to encourage it but he decided this would be home from now on. He was cheeky, likeable, unafraid and demanded food and attention. We thought he may have been abandoned so I called him Dumped. He liked to sit on my lap while I trundled round in the electric wheelchair but he was a fierce hunter rather than a pussycat!

Although I was strengthening up slowly, it was still taking me a week or more to get over a day or night out but that never stopped me from accepting invitations. I only declined if they were too close together. I loved going to various do's; they were mainly racing orientated and made me feel alive even though I felt and looked nearly dead afterwards! I revelled in being amongst the racing crowd. It was what I knew about and I could converse about something that interested me. They talked and treated me the same as before I adopted the wheelchair. I was given the chance to look forward and get on with life whilst treasuring my most memorable racing days with pride, and that was very important. For my head and thoughts, my personality, my wicked sense of humour and resilience, were still all of me but the only thing some people saw were my arms and legs that didn't work. Doom, gloom and tragedy. Yes, there had been a calamity but I resented being spoken to as if I was a child and, in my case, what you saw was not what you got! Unfortunately, it was my mum who became the main sufferer as I had to prove I was not helpless and, even though I loved her dearly, I was continually mean and sharp. If she said I shouldn't have been on that horse once, she said it a thousand times. I became more irate because of her doubt at my ability. I didn't want to be mollycoddled or have to deal with her emotion and I thought if she saw how strong I was it would make her strong too.

But there was one weak link in my armour, one piece of yesterday that rendered me feeble. So in November '92, when everything had been sorted out with TC and the remnants of his belongings and our life together had been packed neatly into boxes and taken away, I decided not to see him anymore. I would miss him, he had been my very best friend – ever. He told me to be brave and if I ever needed anything I only had to call. I knew that I would often need him but I would never call him and would never watch him walk away from me again... and, "oh yes, I would be brave." I was an emotional and physical wreck.

I would seem to be coping; I would seem to be brave; but inside I raged and cried out. I inwardly mourned for my love and lost limbs; it was the only way, and when it was all over I knew I would never hurt like this ever again...

Christmas was soon upon us and now it was my turn to make an effort. Even though my handwriting, achieved by a pen fixed into a strap and tied around my hand, was still scribble, I signed all my Xmas cards and that made me feel good. I knew that some people may not realise they were from me but it would not take a lot of working out. I think they were appreciated. The house looked good inside and out, mum and Uncle Michael had been down at regular intervals throughout the year to do every kind of job imaginable. The place was filled with warmth, love and the merriment that it had lacked sometimes through the year but now I was visibly lifted by those close to me and the unexpected callers who also had made the effort.

The round garden table and chairs were scrubbed and brought in for dinner to be served. Jennie and Bryn joined us and for a moment I thought about the Wrekin ward. All those other people experiencing the same misfortune. I wondered how Sam (the monster) was getting on; if she could make a new life at only seventeen then I had no cause to complain. We had written to each other once but we didn't keep it up. I knew a few of them kept in touch with each other from a girl called Venetia, who was in at the same time as us. She had broken her back while living in Cyprus and was now having difficulty finding somewhere to live. I knew I had been extremely lucky in returning to my own home and I appreciated more than ever the Christmas scene in my lounge. Television on, bright paper scattered on the floor, the smell of delicious cooking wafting through and a Croft Original sherry on the rocks. The new year dawned and brought with it the reality of how I was going to spend the rest of my days. I was adjusting.

The Injured Jockeys' fund is a marvellous charity and I hope all the other sports look after their people as well. I may have been gone but certainly not forgotten. One of the Trainers, Jack Berry, whose son Sam suffered a head injury in the '80s, raised money so a group of ex-jockeys with various injuries could go on holiday to Tenerife. It was to a complex in Los Cristianos, specially designed to cater for wheelchairs. It sounded wonderful, with heated swimming pool, warm sun, plenty of vino tinto and all in the middle of freezing old February. But I was slightly apprehensive. Anyway, before I found a viable excuse not to go, I was at the airport. Of course it was different and of course silly little things were done that upset me but I apportioned the blame to the ignorance of the hurrying natives who were responsible for manhandling me. A good holiday was enjoyed by all, which included my sister, Justine, Janet, who was now working more hours, and a fairly new girl, Tracy, who had replaced Becky when she had to leave.

Carey joined us full time and it seemed amazing that I needed so many people to take care of me. Later on in the year I was sorry to see Petra leave but she had decided to start a family and return to her native Sweden. I didn't have any trouble finding someone else and I was pleased that a lady called Joan who had been coming at weekends was happy to join us.

I was eager to get on and do something worthwhile. I could not spend the rest of my life doing nothing. At the start of the flat season I began to keep a record of the points table and every lady who rode in a race in Britain for the Lady Jockeys' Association. I used my left finger peg, that I also used when reading the newspaper, to tap out the relevant information on my Mark (I'll show you how to work it properly next week) Madgwick computer. Some things never change! Twenty minutes' work would take me the best part of an afternoon and I was only copying. This made me realise how feeble I was. It gave me little satisfaction, and even less on a bad day when I wished I was out there with them.

A few people had suggested I write a book or do something with my poems (that I had been writing since my teenage days) and, after toying with the idea for a while, I met Terry Norman, who worked for the *Sporting Life*, at Lydia's Champion Lady Jockeys' luncheon. After a few discussions I thought one day, how could anyone else write about my life, no one else could write about my feelings. I wrote the first page and Terry told me to carry on. And I did – when I wasn't complaining about neck or shoulder pain, my position in the chair making a big difference to my concentration. I felt as if I was doing something, even if it was only for a few hours a week. At first it was just a hobby, a pastime, then it became a dream and eventually a challenge. I realised how uneducated I was and had to admit my spelling was atrocious, my grammar diabolical and my English "not right proper". Like my first ride, it couldn't get any worse! Give up; never...

It was nice to be 'phoned up out of the blue and in Richard Phillips I had found a good friend. I didn't know Richard to talk to before, even though he had been an assistant trainer and racing impersonator (of trainers and jockeys). He had now joined the training ranks so it was particularly interesting for me to have some horse talk as well as a giggle. Carey was left in the bar at the Guineas meeting in May, whilst Richard and I slipped round the racecourse, giving our expert opinion on horse, rider, spectator and commentator! It was great for me not to have to explain where to go all the time and have the chair placed near enough to see the horses but far enough away for safety. We heard the thunder and watched the lightning strike before the big black imposing figure of *Zafonic* strode up the hill to take the Two Thousand Guineas and I delighted in the fact that I was there with such an amusing friend.

By the summer my life was ticking over okay. I seemed to be busy doing nothing, well it felt like nothing. I didn't know where I was going and, all of a sudden, I realised I had no aim. It had all been about recovering as much as possible but, as the two-year marker passed, I felt I needed some discipline in my life, some stimulation. My hours at the computer were met with an uninterested insubordination and the more people said one thing, the more I did the opposite. Awkward little sod! My sarcastic and witty remarks rose to an all time high and I actually thought I was being humorous. I was very bored, amusing myself wickedly at the expense of others until it was no longer funny, too one-sided. This behaviour was the only outlet for the mountain of frustration building up inside me. It was seeing girls dressed in shorts or petite dresses, it was not being able to frolic in the sun, it was about feeling a social outcast, it was about being unattractive, abandoned. It was the vivid dreams, night after night, that saw me walking, running, riding, being held – loved. It was about everything I was now and everything I had been, and I could say I was still the same person as before until I was blue in the face but I wasn't, was I? I was handicapped, disabled, wheelchair bound... Depression? I don't think so, or maybe I just didn't recognise it. I kept holding on to my past life, clinging onto the memories, afraid that they would fade away and then I would have nothing left that was mine. I didn't want to upset or burden my family and friends, I had to do this by myself. I was sharing my life with strangers and I was a very private person. I may have thought I was going nowhere and that living a satisfying life was over for me but I couldn't really believe that, it was not in my nature. I didn't give up, did I? That is how I got here in the first place!

September '93, just over two years since my fall, and still the stinging and burning feeling in my arms persisted. At times I despaired as I looked out of the window, longing to be free again whilst a raging infection saw me rest my head on the desk top. I'd screw my face up trying to fight off the pain and frustration...

But it would never ever beat me...

And this was the challenge to start again, to sort it out. The torch was there, it just needed me to put the batteries in!

Not Always

OoO

I haven't always been this way
you know
It used to be me that went out at night
Did my own hair, led the fast life
It used to be me that did all the chores
They used to be mine
And now they are yours
I haven't always been this way
you know
It was me who had all the
get up and go
It was me who polished and hoovered round
It was me who danced late
one night
And me in bright pink shell suit
Who ran till I was out of
sight
I haven't always been this way
you know
It was me who had the lawn
to mow
Chop the wood and hang the clothes
And I who did the garden
hoe
I haven't always been this way
you know
And now I put my trust in you
To do the things
I used to do
Not always have I been this way
You know

OoO

Sharron Murgatroyd

CHAPTER FIFTEEN

So Much to Do, So Much to See,
So Much to Live For

I'd never realised how beautiful the Autumn could be. My life had been so blinkered and now I was opening up to a multitude of sights and sounds. The green changing to shiny reddish brown of the leaves in the tree-lined wooded dip just before the horse crossing to the Limekiln gallop on the Bury Road was an array of colour and splendour. I wondered why I hadn't noticed it before in all the years driving from Kennett to Newmarket.

Time had also arrived for a few changes to the house. The old greenhouse and garage were well past their sell-by date. With the help of Neville, an architect, who was a friend of Nancy and Alan Chamber's who lived in the village, we discussed a few changes. Work was soon under way and, as in the past, I had my say in why, which and wherefore. Ron, who had built the stables, was again chief brickie, his work second to none. My dining room would eventually be just that again, my bedroom would become an office and, with a new bedroom, bathroom and so called gym, my life and that of my lady helpers would be pretty luxurious.

I had been more than lucky to keep my home. I loved it – I had always loved it. After Becky had gone I knew I never wanted another live-in. I felt a strange feeling of contentment in the couple of hours that I managed to be alone – sometimes in complete silence and other times with music so loud the poor old house fairly trembled with vibrancy. I often wandered around looking in each room, looking out of the windows. I once spent a whole unplanned hour in the hallway. After one of the girls went home, I decided to wander whilst I waited for Jennie and Bryn to come round. I was glad to hear Bryn's voice, "Where are you?"

"I'm here."

"What are you doing there?" he said laughing.

"I've run out of batteries." It happened a lot to start with. There was no gauge on the old red chair, and I could be found stranded in various places inside and outside Becklyn. My worst time was at the end of the drive; all these people I knew kept driving past giving me a toot and a wave. I felt a right divi. I couldn't even wave back!

I had a new career to find for myself and I knew it would not come to me. I was still ambitious to do something, I could not sit and vegetate; I would not! Living on yesterday soon becomes stale as everybody else moves on. My poems had really only ever been for myself, mum and the odd close friend, so I didn't really envisage them being a factor. I smiled, remembering the raucous laughter one night as Tina Brisbourne, with Joss and myself as a captive audience, recited her jolly ditties. I, on the serious side, recited a few verses. There was one in particular that I thought would tug at their heart strings. It was about picking up stones from a field bare and barren, very meaningful. I heard muffled sounds and looked up expecting to see them with their hankies out but instead they were creased up in their respective chairs, hands trying to hide screwed-up faces that now exploded into uncontrollable laughter. "Do you think you could try and write a happy one?" they managed to say.

The book was still at nursery stage and didn't look like getting to primary. I had liked writing stories but that was in my teenage years, although I had started one after my broken heart and before my broken neck! I giggled to myself, Alison and Jen will like that. Or perhaps I could be an Assistant Trainer? Sean Woods' office desk did suit me rather well. No, I wanted to be my own boss, for now I was going power crazy! Trainer? The yard needed a lot of work to finish it off and I wasn't quite ready for that with no backing. Jockeys' agent? Didn't really fancy it but I could have my arm twisted.

I was like a small fish in the ocean and a new career in racing would not be easy to find. I thought of the careers teacher all those years ago flicking over the cards of various jobs. I scolded myself for being so naive and not preparing myself more academically, although I don't suppose a jockey is really bothered as to how well he'd do on Mastermind as he kicks a big green novice chaser into the open ditch – as long as common sense prevails and reasons with the guts of both horse and rider! Anyway, with the magical experience and rush of adrenalin that you feel, who really cares? There is always tomorrow. Tomorrow was here for me, a shade premature by my reckoning but nevertheless here it was.

The loss of a sponsor for a ladies' hurdle race at Market Rasen was unfortunate and Sandy Brooks, the secretary for the Lady Jockey's Association (LJA), asked me if I had any ideas. If I could find a sponsor, liaise with the Clerk of the Course for complimentary tickets and whatever else to make an enticing package, then I would be doing something worthwhile. It would also see me back amongst the action. I was straight onto the case, ringing up only to be met with, "Love to but not there, maybe somewhere else, some other time." I mentioned it in conversation to my brother Mark and then wondered if they would like a day at the races. My two brothers used to work for my dad in double glazing. I rarely spoke to or saw my dad. When he did ring, more often than not it was on a bad day and my conversation was limited to yes or no! Anyway, in spite of that, he was my dad and did want to do something to help. I suppose better late than never. His company was well publicised when he sponsored four ladies' races but

I'm afraid our relationship went from bad to worse. It was mostly my fault, as I felt our contact was a deep-seated betrayal to my mother and didn't feel comfortable in his company and that of his friends.

I felt akin with my new little venture to start with but soon became disappointed as, after initial contact, things were then taken out of my hands. I felt I was being patronised. "Poor little Sharron, give her something to do – not too much, though!" Or was I just not up to the job? Well I gave it a go, satisfied just to cover my expenses, but unfortunately I didn't. With most of the work being done on the telephone or fax, it suited me but with that and paying a driver to get me to the meetings, not to mention overtime for my own girl who attended me, I was soon spending more than I could afford to. My first payment of twenty pounds hardly stretched to lunch and drinks. My next payment never arrived. And I thought I was dealing with gentlemen who ran the racecourses, or maybe the wires got crossed somewhere along the way. There were three good results, though, that made me feel like I had done something right. Gee Armytage rode a great race to win the first ladies-only chase at Wetherby but the turn out of only four runners was a bit disappointing. Later on in the summer Jennie rode the opposition into the ground when she won on *Visimotion* at Thirsk. One of the most satisfying was organising a race at Yarmouth for Dodson and Horrell, which Di Jones won. John Sharp left me to do all the arrangements and I was well pleased when I covered my expenses. The once popular ladies' races were becoming increasingly difficult to find and keep new sponsors for, as was the Championship. It seemed a shame but, as time moves on, the riders themselves need to be more aware that promoting themselves is just as important as getting the rides.

I was plugging on slowly with my book which was starting to take shape. I looked back on my life poignantly and enjoyed remembering the things I had done. Coley Road had been an idyllic place to spend ones childhood. I had enjoyed being seventeen, they were fun-loving carefree days, and my twenties had been fuelled with ambition and love. I had also written a small piece about the experience of my holiday abroad and one about going racing to Newmarket on a July evening. I was beginning to enjoy writing a few of my thoughts down and they were just for me – private. I amused myself by setting up a file and everytime I felt a bit of a grievance I'd have a moan to the computer. It was a pity that it could not respond but I always felt better afterwards!

The stark reality brought about by a game of Trivial Pursuit made me fall into the dumb and dumber category. I began to read more and generally tried to sharpen up. I had let my brain become very lazy and certainly needed to broaden my horizons. The last book I'd read had been a smutty beach time filler but now I wanted to read and learn significant things. There was so much about lots of things I did not know. I already admired the talents of Richard Dunwoody and Adrian Maguire in racing but now I was taking in a wide range of talents and admired Sally Gunnell and Colin Jackson in athletics. The dedication of Torville and Dean and music that ranged from Meat Loaf to Take That was all so different but was all so pleasurable. I liked to watch the Formula 1 racing and had always liked to watch Wimbledon. I admired the girls that sailed in the round-the-world yacht race. I cheered for everyone who was about to achieve anything. I had become an avid fan of *Racing Post* columnist Paul Haigh and Brough Scott's diary, noting that I would never be able to emulate their kind of writing if I lived until I was a hundred.

I had become very independent, even of my friends. This was mainly due to a good set of staff that emerged. I didn't want my friends to feel as if they had to do anything for me out of a sense of duty. I wanted them to see me because they wanted to, not because I needed something doing. After a long week they might not feel like going racing, so I was now able to make my own arrangements. It was hard work at first, though, and especially if my helper was far from interested in horses of any shape or form. It was as life is, forever moving on. I felt sometimes I was being left behind but it really was good for me because we have to live our own lives and everyone wants or needs something different. I was soon moving in a different direction, while still maintaining my valued friendships with Joss, Jennie and Alison.

I had been accosted by a lady in Newmarket one day asking me if I would be interested in going to the local Driving for the Disabled group. Sue Ram, the group organiser, was obviously very keen for me to go and a couple of people had mentioned that I might find it fun. Jogging about in a pony and trap was hardly going to compensate for the riding but now with my "new attitude" I decided to give it a go. I went along to Mrs Reeder's place at Worlington. *Winston* is a fine looking grey and is more horse-looking than pony. The traps are a good size, too. I didn't fancy being pulled round by a little pony looking like we'd just jumped out of the Thelwell book. I was pushed up the metal ramps in the wheelchair and placed upsides Sue Ram. My first impression was that of joy. I was on the same level as her, I felt on equal terms and, for the first time in what seemed like an age, I now looked down towards those standing on the ground. The horse stood between the shafts and, even though I wasn't on his back, as the reins were fastened round my wrists and I felt the tug of his soft mouth, the contact was magical. If I had closed my eyes I could have been back in the saddle. This would never be a substitute for race riding and nobody was asking it to be, it was a totally different sport and it deserved respect.

Driving could be very frustrating as I had great difficulty sitting up straight and comfortable. Even though I was strapped into my chair I kept falling over to the left. Luckily, my instructor sat on that side so she could give me a shove back. We tried all sorts of rolls and cushions but it was still a lot to do with my weak body. My middle just caved in. It was early days, though, and some weeks filled me with more enthusiasm than others.

At Becklyn the bungalow and garden were tidy and the new garage matched the stable block. It replaced the old shanty-town-looking one, that had adjoined the shabby greenhouse (which had now been done away with) and now looked very smart. It was hard to imagine how it had been back in 1986: wild but still lovable, and how it had been transformed from market garden into an adequate private equestrian establishment. The dark railed paddock that had been sectioned off into small, medium and large also had a woodchip lunge ring, where I had spent a lot of time riding, bringing on young horses or simply keeping it tidy. But since Maureen, John and *Della* had moved away, and with no one to take care of *Fiefdom* (he had landed a nice little winter job being Sean Woods' hack), the ten stables and half-finished yard were looking shabby and unkempt. The top end that had never been finished was an eyesore and the lunge ring had become overgrown with weeds. When I looked out of my office window it was an empty, desolate, lifeless scene. I knew something had to be done but it was easier to ignore.

I didn't think for one minute that I would ever see the young man, who knocked at my door one Saturday afternoon, again. He enquired about the land that surrounded my property and did I know who owned it? He was looking for somewhere to start up schooling and bringing on showjumpers and eventers. He had done quite a lot of eventing. I didn't think there was much call for it as racing ruled in this area. I did know who owned the land but it was very doubtful if he would sell any of it. We had asked a long time ago but he was holding out for planning permission. It was a few weeks later when my mum took a call from a Mr Young, who said he had bought the piece of land that adjoined mine at the far end of the unfinished yard, and if I wondered what was going on, they were just up there clearing the rubbish, ragwort and generally tidying up.

I could see the activity from the office window and trundled up the paddock. My offer of a lager made me an instant hit with Mr Young and his brother-in-law, who introduced themselves as Andy and Russell. Andy has become a good friend and made a very adequate schooling area for jumping and dressage on his land. He also motivated me into finishing off my yard. We have been an enormous help to each other and while that end of my life was hiding because I didn't have the help or inclination to do anything about it, now he has breathed life back into it. It has a different life, with me there only to observe and offer advice, but nonetheless life it now has. His suggestion that we run a concrete strip between the two properties, for horse and wheelchair access only, was a good idea; I can watch him giving tuition or riding if I want to, and if I keep quiet!

It was marvellous to watch the progression that Darren (who also became a new friend) made with his riding, and although I must admit to feeling a little envious as I watched him ride *Fiefdom* in the paddock, it also gave me pleasure. But with all this activity and long discussions about eventing (my first trip to Burghley where Janet and Andy deserved a medal for pushing me round) and comparing it with racing, going to the pub with Andy and his wife Dawn, Darren with his wife Emma and keeping a strong contact with my other friends, I wasn't doing much work on this book!

For three months I helped Terry Kent, who rode jumping for Julie Cecil, as his agent but although he rode a few winners for Alan Bailey, I didn't feel I could do much to help him. My mornings did not start early enough and I soon became disheartened as I could not get him on the rides I was ringing up for, some of which were winning, whilst being careful not to step on anybody's toes, as this part of the jumping game I knew all too well.

My new partners in crime were Andy and Darren. I say crime for, when grilled about whose fault it was that we had stayed in the Bell until closing time instead of just half an hour, after Darren had had a riding lesson, we all blamed each other. I think they often went home with slightly squiffy halos on and the convenient M (martyr) on their forehead, saying I had been enjoying myself so much they hadn't wanted to take me home too early! Andy was interested in buying a young horse to bring on and I suggested that he might be able to pick up a three- or four-year-old from the October Horses In Training sale. Darren became interested too and, on my advice, they bought a lovely three-year-old filly called *Paddock Talk*. She had run once in a flat race and the first time she was presented at ground poles, she popped over well. As she progressed I wanted to have her and I also wanted to ride her but as neither of these two things were possible, she was eventually moved on. After all that had happened I found myself still becoming attached to horses, still loving and showing understanding, still not wanting to let go, even now when I could only watch from the sidelines. And guess what? Yes, she was chestnut with a white face! An ideal friend for *Fiefdom*, too.

I had been very lucky with what I call my team of ladies. The youngest girl, Tracy, at twenty-three, with hair shorn and nose pierced, took some flak and rollickings but they mostly went over her head. After two years we both needed a change and, after going part-time for a while, I persuaded her to try a nannie's job in America and broaden her horizons. She tells me she is very happy. Carey worked for me full-time then on a part-time basis and was very versatile but a better opportunity came along and I'm all for that. I know I can call upon her if needs be. So now, Nancy is still the chief cook (unless my mum is here), and Petra, who is now sometimes accompanied by her two-year-old son, Jake, (and soon to be leaving again for baby number two), shares duties with my main ladies, Janet and Joan. They have made my life easy and normal with the minimum of fuss and often put themselves out to suit me. When we set out for the odd day trip, holiday or weekend away, as the last few items are put in the car I laugh and say, "Come on, it's like going away with the Brighton Belles!" It all works very well as now I'm at a stage where they can drop me off at a party or function with my friends and return at my request. The Jockeys' Christmas Party at the Sudbury House Hotel, Farringdon was fantastic. It was like being out on my own and I received even more attention than ever before!

My New Year's resolution was to discipline myself and make it my job to finish the book. I split the days up, working round the physio and horse and trap. After reading the papers in the morning, I'd try to do two or three hours work then have a break, then get on and do some more. I definitely worked better when I was left completely alone but sometimes I would sit staring into space not knowing what to put next. One day when I was in a productive working mood, Rob Pilsworth, one of the vets from Rossdale's veterinary practice, whom I had known since my days at Alan Bailey's, called in to see me. "What are you up to?" he said and I told him I was writing my autobiography. "Oh yeh," he said, not very interested. I asked if he would like to read the first chapter. "Yeh," he said, still not very interested. After sitting and reading it he was quite surprised that I could string three words together! He asked if he could show it to one of his colleagues, Peter Rossdale, who had an interest in a publishing company and had published veterinary books in the past. I agreed to this as I felt a professional opinion would be helpful. It was. Rob had set the wheels in motion. Peter Rossdale became my agent, he loaned me his assistant, Brigitte Heard, and also recruited his dear friend, Ian Wallace, singer and writer, to read my manuscript and give his opinion on my writing. I was very surprised it got the thumbs up, and it gave me plenty of encouragement! It made the hours that I had been sitting alone, tapping away monotonously and sometimes wondering why, a little more worthwhile. I had a goal now; I had involved other people and it would have to be realised.

In early February I went on my second Injured Jockeys' holiday to Tenerife. While I was there I wrote a piece about the holiday and it was published in the *Sporting Life* on my return. I was now being motivated by my writing. This became my new work, my horse and trap was my new sport, I still loved my racing and my social life was first-rate. My life was full; what more could I ask for?

There was one thing I could ask for – the full recovery of my friend Alison Thom. She had to undergo surgery to remove a brain tumour, which was then found to be malignant, and through the summer she would have to endure a course of radiotherapy. All of a sudden the roles were reversed; my life was content and she was living through a trauma. So now it was me who sometimes didn't know what was the right thing to say. But we are friends and wrong words, if any, were brushed away, forgotten. Real friends stick together. I cancelled my annual BBQ; Alison would be in hospital and so would Joss, who suffered horrendously with rheumatoid arthritis but she never complained either.

Brigitte and I worked well together, even after I found out that, because of her, I had been left one very cold day at Bangor (my first visit in 1989). I thought my lift with jockey Vince Smith and his father John was brilliant. That was until, well into our journey, Vince realised I was in the last race. "I've got to be away before the last. I've got a hot date. I didn't realise you was in the last race," he blurted out.

"Don't worry, I'll get a lift home in the horsebox," I replied. Now I was working with the 'hot date' responsible for me getting a lot of earache off the stable lad and box driver, Tommy Strang, whom I had worked with in my Dickinson days, for being beaten a head and a short-head into third place. I forgave her but Vince never hears the last of it! When I was too fatigued to type or suffering with sore shoulders, I would dictate to her. I had written about seven chapters and obviously they needed reading through and correcting, big time! Joss offered to help and we had many a good laugh at my poor English but as time went on the improvement was quite clear, even to me.

My lifestyle had certainly changed direction and sometimes I felt as if I was two different people, without bordering on schizophrenia! I had grown up but still retained my humour, using it now more appropriately. I felt more knowledgeable but could feel frustrated at not being able to put to much use what I had soaked up about horses and racing since I was sixteen. It was hard watching other people being busy. Until now it had been great to have someone else doing all the chores but I suppose this feeling of well being brought with it a return to want to cook my own food in my own kitchen. I even wanted to wash up! Instead I turned the music up, wrote for as much of the day as I could stand (sit) comfortably, in between the many interruptions that were welcomed. I fell in love with Bon Jovi for a short while and tried harder than ever to perfect my dressage à la horse and trap.

My first show was at Waltham Abbey where, thanks to Andy, I wore the correct attire. He provided me with soft leather gloves, silk neck stock and tie pin. If I was going to compete at any level, I was going to do it right. It was a showing class judged on horse, trap and driver turn-out. I drove another grey, *Allegro* (my nickname for him is *Ali Pali*), and that day he decided to be a souped-up one. With my co-driver, Mrs Reeder, taking most control we were placed third and, contrary to rumour, there were more than three in the class. Next was Boughton House Trials where, in the Dressage arena, our performance was FFP which means Fairly F...... Pathetic. This is often used in racing terms and not always just about the horse! *Ali Pali* thought he was a fuel injected GTI on this particular day and not the usual 1300 that he is at home. Anyway, to finish last was not too worrying as our precision and time racing through the cone course saved us from being totally "Tailed off!" I couldn't get any worse, honestly, I could not get any worse! Give up? Never.

My second place at the local Animal Health Trust Show was a shade better for another showing class and I felt pleased when I looked around to see some friends had turned up to watch me. As we went into Autumn I began to feel a lot stronger. The stronger I became the more enthusiastic I was. I like the rough and tumble of the cross-country, and speeding through gateways on undulating ground is much more fun than dressage, but if my new ambition and dream is to be realised, I will have to compose myself and put in many, many hours of dedicated practice in dressage. This will be with Andy (my biggest critic) who is on the course to be an "Able Body Whip," so that he is qualified to drive with me. Thanks to the understanding of his wife, Dawn, and their children, Elliot and Rebecca, I may achieve my goal... It is a possibility that for the first time ever, horse and carriage driving could be included in the Para-Olympic Games in the year 2000. We will be working and looking forward to it; with hope.

Towards the end of Autumn I had a burning desire to get back onto a horse. Maybe it was because of the press reports of Declan Murphy's successful comeback to riding after being on the brink of death, and my friend Gee Armytage getting back into the saddle after her bad fall, where she broke two vertebrae in her back. How would it be achieved and when would it happen? I didn't know; all I knew was that I had this strong feeling inside me.

Andy and Petra definitely thought I was joking and, if it came to it, would this desire still be there? It did, and it was. Three days later, on Saturday November 4th 1995, it happened – with the help of Andy, Janet, Jenny and Mick Cornwell, their daughter Michelle, Emma, who had ridden out *Fiefdom*, and a young girl who ended up with a camera thrust into her hand. In one fell swoop I was lifted from wheelchair onto *Fiefdom*'s back, secured by many hands, then, positioned with my head to one side of his neck, I could stroke and feel him with my left hand. His soft coat next to my cheek was very endearing. Andy was gently legged up to ride pillion and hold me into a proper riding position. He held a very elated but unsteady friend; a smile and the familiar feeling that compressed four years and three months into only yesterday. As the song goes, "Did you think I would leave you crying, when there's room on my horse for two? Climb up here and don't be sighing, he can go just as fast with two!!" Somehow a ghost has been laid to rest; I know I can get on my *Fiefdom* if I wish and, as I write about it, I am content to be able to do just that.

I miss the romance that two people can share and I know I will never be in love again but I don't think that's because of my immobility. It's because I'm an "awkward little sod", which could be misinterpreted as being selfish. But not having to consider another person and being left to my own devices for so long has made me this way.

It gives me great pleasure to see other people enjoying themselves but I know most don't appreciate their lives. You only realise how important a toss of the head or a stretch of the leg is when you can't do it anymore. There is so much to love and so very much to miss. Nobody seems totally happy with their lot and I can understand that. My experience has brought me great depths of fortitude and an outlook on life that is completely different from how it was before. Without the accident I wonder if I would have become so aware of how wonderful life can be, how much there is to do and see, outside of my obsession with racing. Or would I have stayed unhappy with my lot – always striving for more, ignorant of how precious a walk in the rain by oneself can be?

It is with gratitude I treasure my past life, not blaming or questioning it, not wanting to trade it in with anybody else – then or now. There is an amazing difference between physical and emotional pain; both dig deep trying to destroy your soul but both can be dealt with. To put 110 per cent into something means that there have to be sacrifices. So while a second chance to live a fully mobile and physically normal life would be met with the euphoria to top all, I can still embrace the rest of my life with knowledge and more understanding. I tell myself, "It was just meant to be..."

I have laid a ghost to rest by getting on my *Fiefdom*. We shall never canter nor gallop, he and I, for the fences I face now are different and the course is very long.

Give up? Never... "Jump Jockeys Don't Cry".

That which does not kill me
Makes me stronger...

OoO

Friedrich Wilhelm Nietzsche

Racing Bye...

OoO

I don't want to sit here anymore
Trying to write
I want to be out there
I want to ride
Go racing with the boys
Be upsides
Be in the race and kick again
In all weathers
With the men
Make the pace
Too fast too slow
Jump the first and settle in
Champagne for after
If you win
Top jockey will take your place
If you lose
I can handle that
It's what I choose
Jockey shouts at you sailing by
Bloody women
They love us but we make them cry
Smell the turf So wet
So green
Another win
Me and my horse are such a good team
The glow from inside
That feels so warm
An inner satisfaction
Is emotional for all
You hope it never ends
But it's cold when you fall
Pick yourself up
Brush yourself down
Because you want more
From a cheering crowd
Your Jockey friend he's won a race
You feel so proud
We always celebrate
But triumph and disaster
Lie side by side
My trainer finds me
To say
My beloved horse has died
And our tears are not shallow
For the heroes we ride
We know it could be us

But we push those thoughts
Aside
And better to have tasted some glory
Somewhere
Than hidden in a corner
Never to have dared
The winter night draws in
Crowds make their way home
They have shared a little emotion
But they haven't shared it all
Breeches, boots and belongings
Packed tightly into bags
Where are you tomorrow?
Sit down
Have a fag
Jockeys' room nearly empty
Bright colours all faded away
Only valets and stragglers left
Reflecting on what might have been
What has happened
Today
The boys are all ready
Early elation now in hand
Two winners and a fall
On the Southwell sand
Saddles and bags we carry
Mobile phone to explain
Happy and forlorness
As we drive away
One empty space in the car
Jockey won't be travelling home
But he's not badly hurt
This time we tell his wife
Just a little sore
And some of our heroes
Won't be home tonight
But we all know what they have been
The actors on centre stage
So we can live our dream
I don't want to sit here anymore
But that's the way it has to be
Because one day
Jockey
Didn't come home
While trying to live her dream

OoO

Sharron Murgatroyd

Acknowledgements

I have finished this book but feel I still have so much to say. The thank-yous spread far and wide and I know that the people who are closest to me often feel that I am ungrateful. I am not; so please forgive me if I sometimes seem that way. My bossy behaviour, I know, is very annoying but in my own defence my voice is now doing the job of two arms and two legs; it is just unfortunate that you – the people who are my family, my friends and my forever loyal ladies – have in effect taken over the part they used to play!

For the people who have been part of my life in the past, there may be silence now between us but at the time, when I needed support, you gave it to me and I thank you; even if I was in your thoughts for only one moment of the day. For the complete strangers who wrote words of encouragement and made me feel just that little bit special, you may not all be mentioned but you will never be forgotten. Thank you to those of you who, however busy you are, find the time to telephone just to say "hello"; and the visits are warming, gifts are not necessary.

Thank you to the doctors, nurses, physios and everyone else who shared Wrekin Ward at the Robert Jones and Agnes Hunt Orthopaedic Hospital Gobowen Shropshire, from August 2nd 1991 – February 14th 1992 for their care and advice. These have definitely helped me cope with my new way of life.

And thank you to all the people who have helped and encouraged me in their own way to achieve the end of this work.

My faith has baffled me since I was a young child. Is there a God? I do not pray but there must be footprints in the sand!

Footprints in the Sand

OoO

One night I had a dream. I was
walking along the beach with the
Lord, and across the skies flashed
scenes from my life. In each scene,
I noticed two sets of footprints in the
sand. One was mine and one was the
Lord's. When the last scene of my life
appeared before me, I looked back at the
footprints in the sand and, to my surprise,
I noticed that many times along the path
of my life there was only one set of footprints.
And I noticed that it was at the lowest
and saddest times in my life.
I asked the Lord about it:
"Lord, you said that once I decided
to follow you, you would walk with me
all the way. But I notice
that during the most troublesome times
in my life there is only one set of footprints.
I don't understand why you left my side
when I needed you most."
The Lord said:
"My precious child. I never
left you during your time of trial.
Where you see only one set of footprints,
I was carrying you."

OoO

Author unknown